Praises for Schlopping

"I just love it. *Schlopping* is heartwarming, interesting, and funny. It is written and organized in a magical way that brings the experiences and family alive to the reader."

–Barbara Rosenstein, author of *English with Interest*

"*Schlopping* catches the essence of the relationships between generations who bonded and more importantly shared during artfully disguised shopping episodes. Many moments are embedded in stores: from Christmas displays, to tag sales, just browsing, and catching glimpses of life. All parents of teen-agers should read the wisdom shared by the mother-daughter team and learn from their honestly described experiences."

–Marikim Bunnell, M.D., Brigham and Women's Hospital

"A wonderful book that uncovers in the mundane the deepest secrets and the deepest joys flowing between mothers and daughters; well-told and well-crafted."

–Rabbi Joseph Polak, author of *After the Holocaust the Bells Still Ring*

"*Schlopping* reminds us that the strongest family bonds, entwined with small intimate moments, shared ordinary activity and plenty of affection, can sustain and uplift a family through life and beyond."

–Michael Levy, frequent contributor to the Jewish Blog,
"The New Normal"

Schlopping™

Schlⱺpping™

(noun)

schlep + love + shopping

Developing Relationships, Self-Image & Memories

Sheryl E. Mendlinger, Ph.D. & Yael Magen, Esq.
Illustrations by Roxie Voorhees

Me & Ma, Co. Boston 2014

Cover Design by Roxie Voorhees
Book Design by Tanya Wlodarczyk
Edited by Leslie Brunetta

Library of Congress Cataloging-in-Publication Data

Schlopping
(noun)
schlep + love + shopping

Developing Relationships, Self-Image & Memories

Sheryl E. Mendlinger & Yael Magen

Library of Congress Control Number: 2015902220

Printed edition ISBN 978-0-9909525-0-3
E-book edition ISBN 978-0-9909525-1-0

1. Relationships. 2. Shopping. 3. Mothers and Daughters. 4. Self-image. 5. Life Style. 6. Self-help. 7. Sociology. 8. Parenting. I. Title.

Visit our website at www.schlopping.com

FIRST EDITION

For our grandparents, parents, siblings, spouses,
children, and grandchildren, who have
taught us the lessons of life,
and the love of
Schlopping

Contents

Preface

SCHLOPPING EXAMINES THE RELATIONSHIPS, self-image, and memories that develop while shopping with people we love. This book is for anyone who has a loved one and wants to create positive memories that will last a lifetime.

We—Sheryl and Yael—are descendants of three generations of store owners in Texas, where shopping was our livelihood, existence, and family togetherness. Shopping trips with our family were really schlopping expeditions during which we would spend the day together, schlep from place to place, buy various items, share a meal with giggles and gossip, and just enjoy each other's company. As a result, over a decade ago we created a new word that entered into our family lexicon, *schlopping*, which is a linguistic blend of *schlep* (a Yiddish word which means carrying a heavy load or going from place to place), *love*, and *shopping*. Schlopping is the ritual of schlepping with someone you love while shopping.

This book has evolved over the span of seven years, during which we both completed graduate degrees, experienced and overcame illnesses, and were fortunate to become a grandmother and mother, respectively, twice.

Sheryl is a researcher in women's health and intergenerational knowledge acquisition and has published academic papers on these topics. Yael is a lawyer focusing on multigenerational families and has worked in government and nonprofits for over a decade and was a mayoral candidate at the age of twenty-six.

Schlopping is written from two different perspectives and in two distinct voices, a mother and a daughter, and examines events over the life cycle. For us, schlopping has become a way of thinking—a way we shop that is not only about purchasing new items, but also a way that we develop relationships, love for our family and friends, personal self-images, and lifelong memories.

We wish to thank our families and especially our husbands, mothers, and children for giving us the joy of life, the love of shopping, and the time to write this book.

We hope that you join us on our schlopping adventures and look forward to hearing how you and your loved ones embrace schlopping, for better or for worse. You can contact us or post your own stories on www.schlopping.com, #schlopping, and @schlopping.

Have fun, and remember that life is about experiences, relationships, health, and love.

1. Definition of Schlopping

"Let's go schlopping!"

schlopping *(noun)*
[schlóp-ping]
[**sch**(lep)+ **lo**(ve)+(sho)**pping**] - a linguistic blend
Ritual of schlepping with someone you love while shopping
Ex.: "We schlopped 'til we dropped.";
"We went schlopping yesterday."

SCHLOPPING IS AN ACTIVITY that you do with a loved one that acts as a relationship enhancer; it happens when you decide you want to spend time together with someone you love.

Think about a time when you left your house with a loved one—mother, father, son, daughter, brother, sister, grandparent, best friend, aunt, grandchild—and went from store to store, tried on an endless number of garments, bought dozens of items, stopped for a meal or a drink, and returned home tired and content. You laughed and giggled, you cried and fought, you kissed and hugged and chit-chatted throughout the day.

Shopping is a global phenomenon and research shows that the main motivation is connecting with other human beings. There is something unique about shopping that probably results from the fact that it takes place in a public, neutral place that allows people to forget problems, resolve conflicts, and reinvent themselves.

Schlopping is shopping with the extra ingredient called love. It is schlepping from store to store, with a loved one, to enjoy each other's company. When you schlop, you experience all the feelings on the spectrum of the emotional rainbow, such as excitement, happiness, empowerment, anger, and sadness.

Schlopping is not only about what you buy but also about whom you do it with; it provides the opportunity to enhance relationships, create lifelong memories, and shape the way we view ourselves and the world.

You know you have gone schlopping when you arrive home covered with sweat from the schlep, a heart filled with love, and bags in your hands.

2. Schlopping For Your First Bra: The Budding of the Boobs

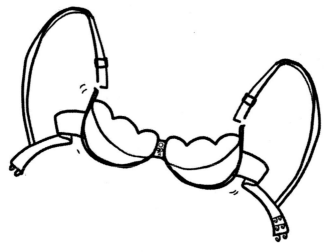

"It's her experience, not yours."

THE RITUAL OF BUYING THE FIRST BRA is one that is often embedded in a young girl's memory. The realization that your body is growing, changing, developing, and slowly becoming a body similar to your mom's is experienced in different ways. There are daughters who are embarrassed about their budding breasts or sprouting of hair and wear baggy clothes to conceal, and those who cherish those moments as milestones to maturity and brag about it with friends, family, and on social media. There are mothers who deal with their daughter's puberty in a very private and intimate way, and those who deal with it openly and publicly and share their daughter's experience with the whole world.

As daughters, we experienced this time in our lives very differently.

Sheryl: The developing breast tissue I had when I was about ten years old may have been only prepuberty flab or perhaps it really was the budding of the boobs, but according to my mother it was not something that should be seen, certainly not through the thin, white nylon blouses that were stylish to wear for Sunday school, synagogue, or other dress-up occasions. In the 1960s, before the internet, there was not a lot of guidance as to what bras one should wear and most of our knowledge about this unknown path was gained through magazines, older sisters (whom I did not have), older cousins (whom I did have), and of course our moms or grandmothers.

I was lucky enough to have had a positive experience seeing older women navigate the "how to" of putting on a bra. I cannot talk about my adolescence, especially developing breasts, without thinking about my mother's and grandmother's boobs and bras. From the time I can remember, my maternal grandmother, Gommie as we called her, always had a "full body"—a 40 D—and when I visited her, she would call me into her bedroom and say, "Help me get this closed." I would fasten the hooks and eyes on the back of the full-length corset and pull as hard as I could while she took deep breaths to help ease the elastic into place. When she wore a regular bra with a girdle, she would jump and wiggle herself around to get the too-small girdle over her full-size hips and waist. At that time, I did not understand why she always wore what seemed to be a smaller size than she really was. Today, I know she wore the smaller size in order to have bigger boobs and smaller hips and waist.

My mother, Evelyn, on the other hand, wore only regular bras and did not need the corset, as her mother did, to make her body look thinner. Although only five feet two, she always had the appearance of a taller woman due to her long, slender torso; her thin, beautiful legs; and her rather large bust line, which remains a 32 D to this day. When she got dressed, she would close the hooks in the front and then turn the bra around, and, in the same way that her mother did, would use her hand to jiggle her boobs into the cups of the bra until they fit in snugly.

So now that my boobs were blossoming, Mom and I went off to our first "schlopping for bra" experience to find the right training bra. I was rather small and the breasts were only little buds, and 28 AA was the correct size. I don't recall all the details—that is, I don't remember where we bought the bra, the color, or what we did on that schlopping trip—but I do remember the excitement of coming home, putting on my first bra, and doing my own "fashion show" while gazing at the new image of my body in the bathroom mirror. Later that evening, when Dad came home from work, the first thing he did was congratulate me and say, "*Mazal Tov.* It's hard to believe my little girl is growing up." Although I was proud of finally getting my first bra, I felt very embarrassed when he acknowledged my changing body.

My mom prepared me in some ways for puberty, and the general attitude in our home was a mixed message of openness yet embarrassment about one's body. Since my boobs were already developing and my grandmother and mother had begun menstruating at ages ten and eleven respectively, my mom felt the need to prepare me at age ten. She gave me "the book," the pads, the sanitary belt that held pads in place prior to adhesives, and the talk about the importance of keeping my body to myself.

The message she projected, which was socially accepted in the 1960s, was that you should not do anything that might excite a boy, including wearing revealing clothes, dancing too close, or allowing a boy to touch your body. As my mom told me when I was eleven years old and my older brother, Sam, had a dance party in our home, "Don't dance too close to a boy, because it will get him excited and he may not be able to control himself." The emphasis was not on my body and sexual development, but rather on how boys might react to my developing body and on their sexuality.

In my house, growing up meant I would be old enough to make decisions for myself. From the time I was about eleven, I always wanted to shave off the dark fuzzy hair from my legs that was often the focus of ridicule from my friends. They used to name-call me "hairy legs," and I begged my mother to let me shave. But my mom always said, "Once you get your period, you can shave your legs." Thus, for me the changes in my body—budding boobs, buying a bra, growth of external hair, and menstruation—all represented maturity and independence. My excitement about my budding breasts and developing body as signs of maturity clashed with my mom's reaction to the same events, conveyed in her messages that I should conceal my body and hide my breasts.

Whenever Yael and I visited family and looked at my mom and Gommie getting dressed and putting on their bras, I always laughed at how they had to close the hooks in the front and jiggle their boobs into their bras. I, on the other hand, when I even wore a bra, always hooked my bra in the back, perhaps because my breasts were so small or because my arms were flexible enough that I could reach the center of my back. When I talked to Yael about boobs and bras, I always talked in a humorous way about how difficult it was to maintain large boobs.

Little did I know that my attitude toward big breasts would affect Yael's body image and puberty experience.

Yael: I was embarrassed when others saw the changing of my body. In my house, it meant it would be the dinner-table conversation and my puberty would be the Hot Topic of the Week, which made me feel like a monkey in the zoo.

My mom, Sheryl, was so open about *everything* and talked about my life, all the time, regardless of who was in the room. The only way to protect myself was to be secretive and not share my experiences with my mom. She never could understand the boundaries between public and private, and I knew that everything I told her would be passed on to my dad and her friends and I would be asked about it the next morning.

When I was twelve years old, a week after my Bat Mitzvah, my dad, my mom, my brother, Yotam, and I were driving in the car to go hiking in the Painted Desert near Tucson, Arizona. Out of the blue, and probably out of boredom, my mom raised her head from her macramé board and said, "I wonder when you're going to get your period? I got it when I was twelve and a half, and my mom got it when she was eleven, and Gommie got it when she was ten. You'll probably get it soon." Needless to say, I was embarrassed and infuriated that she said that in front of my dad and brother in a closed car with nowhere to run or hide. I blushed and became silent, only thinking, "Thank God I didn't tell Mom I actually already got my first period a few months ago." I guess it was easier for me to deal with my puberty alone than it was to deal with it with the entire world. This is a story I have never told my mom up until this moment of writing these words, because I didn't want to hurt her feelings.

A few months after the hike, I had a very painful period with heavy bleeding and did not want to go to ballet class. I finally got up the courage to tell my mom that I had gotten my period, and she tried to give me "the talk." I very emphatically told her that I knew everything already and shrugged her off. As I expected, the next day at the dinner table, with Yotam present, my dad asked me questions about my period. The only way I could deal with it was to scream at my mom, "How could you tell him? I told you not to tell him!" and hysterically run into my bedroom, slam the door, and avoid everyone.

All my life, my hippie mom used to laugh about bras and those who were big-chested. She still reminisces about the time I was four years old and we were both in a dressing room with other women and I pointed to a woman and said, "Mom, she's wearing that." "That" was a bra, and I did not even know the word for it because my mom at that time was proud of going braless. As my body developed, I was embarrassed by my big breasts. Like my grandmother, Savta Evelyn, and great-grandmother, Gommie, I too wore a smaller-size bra. But I wore it not to enhance my body, but to hide it. I remember my mom's sarcastic remarks about my grandmother's big breasts while we visited with her and watched her put on a bra. The message I received was "big boobs are bad and the smaller they are the better." So, in my house, breasts and bras were a source of ridicule or embarrassment rather than a natural part of the body. It was only after I saw my friends' boobs when I was fifteen years old that I realized how beautiful my own boobs were and started to take pride in them.

I was a 32 B by the time I bought my first bra and probably needed one much earlier, but I didn't want to go bra-schlopping with my mom or even tell her about it. I knew I had run out of time and needed to buy a bra when I was thirteen years old and boys in my class kept trying to look down my shirt. At that time, because I was embarrassed about having big breasts, I hid them with a 1980s oversized tie-dye T-shirt and did not allow my mom to see me naked. Although my mom asked me several times if I wanted to go buy a bra, I kept saying I did not need one—because I felt that if I opened that door to her, she would talk about it, and talk about it, and talk about it and I would never hear the end of it. She probably would have planned an elaborate schlopping day with me; and might have even sent out a public notice announcing the date, time, and place to her friends and family; and would have told all the salespeople that this was my first bra and make them congratulate me. As if that was not embarrassing enough, my dad would have started with all his questions, before the schlopping trip, after the schlopping trip, and with Yotam at the dinner table.

At that time, we lived in Israel and I knew that I was going, by myself, to America in the summer to visit family and decided to put the bra-buying off until I was alone with Savta Evelyn. As was typical of all my visits to America, I was destined to go schlopping with her. I knew she would not ask any questions, would be patient, and would not tell my mom anything about it.

We went to a huge mall in Houston, Texas, and spent the day schlopping for various things such as shirts, jeans, dresses, shoes, presents, and other items. During the entire time, I was too embarrassed to actually tell my grandmother that I wanted to buy a bra. I was preoccupied with strategizing how to get a bra without actually saying the words "I need a bra." I kept eyeing the lingerie department every time we passed by it, but never got the guts to tell her I needed a bra. The schlopping day was almost over and we started walking toward the exit of the store. I was afraid I had missed my opportunity. However, as feelings of disappointment came upon my little heart, I got lucky and we passed through the lingerie department. I knew it was now or never, so I said, "I need one more thing," and started walking toward the bra section.

While I was picking out my bras, Savta Evelyn did not say anything. She just allowed me to go through the racks peacefully and quietly at my own pace. Needless to say, I didn't know what I was doing, but I tried my best to conceal my ignorance. It probably took me forty-five minutes to choose a bra, but she never said a word; she just stood there next to me, allowing me to be in my own world, making my own decisions without any distractions. She never knew that that was the first time I had bought a bra. I was always very thankful that I bought my bra with her because she gave me the privacy to buy "just one more thing" and didn't need to share it with all the salespeople in the store.

Everything was secretive with me, but I felt I had no choice. My mom drove me crazy by poking and poking and trying to talk openly about these very personal matters. I felt shameful, especially when she spoke about these issues in front of my dad, brother, and friends. But even when it was just the two of us, I felt ridiculed. I felt her questions made me feel like a monkey in the zoo and didn't want to hear her "advice."

Back then I felt that my mom was not sensitive to me or to my personality. Today, as a grown woman, I understand that she was trying to behave in the way she had wanted her mother to behave towards her and which she thought was the better approach. For my mom, sharing my experience of buying my first bra with a saleswoman would have been joyful and a part of the schlopping experience. For me, this sharing would have been embarrassing and shameful.

I have always hooked my bra in the front and turned it around. Throughout my life, I thought I learned this from my mom, but I now realize I probably learned it from my grandmother. I wonder if it is because my mom never wore a bra when I was young and the first grown woman I saw putting on a bra was my grandmother. Or maybe it is because I was always big-breasted and the only way to fit them right is to jiggle them inside the cups. Perhaps personality traits and the way you wear a bra skip a generation.

Dialogue between Sheryl and Yael, November 2011

Sheryl: As a mother, I dealt with your puberty, femininity, or sexuality in an open and public way because in my home when I was growing up these things were not discussed. Although my mom did prepare me for menstruation, little else about what was happening to my body was ever communicated, and certainly nothing about sex. So when I had you, my daughter, I chose to try to do it differently. I wanted you to have a positive feeling about your changing body and sexual development. As a mother, I thought I was dealing with these issues in a more constructive way by talking openly with you and that you would avoid the embarrassment and secrecy of puberty. I did it the way I would have wanted it, but apparently I did not take into account the way that you are and was not sensitive to your needs. For me as a mother, I felt when you were growing up you were such a private person, and when I wanted to take part in your experience you did not want me in that world of yours.

Yael: It is not that I didn't want you in my world; it is that I didn't want everyone else in my world. I do have to say, Mom, that although I was embarrassed by the way you acted, your strategy worked. I always did love my body, thought of myself as the most beautiful woman alive, and could gaze at my naked body in the mirror for hours. But still, I believe that a more private way of dealing with my changing body would have given me a more positive adolescence experience.

Sheryl: It is amazing to see how even when we try as parents to do things differently from our parents and change our children's experience for the better, sometimes we still make the same mistakes our parents made, just from a different perspective. I, as a mother, wanted to have a more open conversation about puberty with you, my daughter, so that you would not feel shameful about your body, the way I felt at times. Although I remember the feeling of embarrassment when my father commented on my first bra, I let the same thing happen to you. It was only as we wrote this chapter that I understood that my actions and "openness" made you feel the same feelings of embarrassment when your changing body became the open dinner conversation with your dad and Yotam. Unfortunately, I did not learn from my experience and made a similar mistake with you.

Yael: I guess we were both cheated of many mother-daughter experiences throughout my puberty. So how do I do it differently with my daughter, three months old, who at this moment is nursing from my breasts? If I do what I wanted you to do, I would make the same mistakes. How do you think I will deal with it?

Sheryl: I envision you as being open and honest about all aspects of your daughter's journey through adolescence, and probably you will speak privately only to her. However, I also believe that you will want to share with her father, Asaf, all the steps that your daughter will take on the road to maturity. You will not want to deny him the "father experience" and I hope you will find a different and better way to share with her.

Yael: It is not up to me to share her experience with anyone. It is only up to her to share her experiences with whomever she wants, if she wants, and, of course, I hope she will want to confide in me. If she doesn't, I hope that she confides in her father or you.

Schlopping Tips

- When communicating to your child about sensitive issues, think about her personality.
- If she is an open person, discussing her puberty openly may empower her, but get her permission first.
- If she is a private person, an intimate discussion at home is more appropriate.
- Be careful how you portray a topic: humor may be perceived as ridicule and silence as embarrassment.
- Think about your own experiences, but don't forget that the most important factor is your child's character, so act accordingly.
- Always remember: It's her experience, not yours.

3. Mirroring the Dressing Room Talk

"That looks beautiful on you."

THE DRESSING ROOM IS A PLACE that can provoke many sensitivities. It often involves examining our reflection in the mirror. A combination of what we see and tell ourselves we see and what others tell us they see, especially when we were young, develops both our self-image and our self-mirror-monologue. "Self-mirror-monologue" is the way we talk to ourselves while we gaze in the mirror and see our own reflection. It is the presence of the mirror and the examination of ourselves in the dressing room that together wire our self-mirror-monologue program to replay the "dressing room talk" throughout our life.

If the dressing room talk we experience is mostly complimentary about the way we look, there is a higher chance that our self-image and our self-mirror-monologue will be positive. However, if the dressing room talk is mostly negative and criticizes our body shape, it can be detrimental to our self-image and self-mirror-monologue. The dressing room is usually not the place to discuss what is "appropriate" for our body shape and actually can be very harmful; it wires our self-mirror-monologue to always look at "flaws." The backlash, consisting of always trying to find the perfect fit, may be devastating in the long run.

Studies show that many women do not like their bodies and do not like looking at their naked bodies in a full-length mirror. The question is: Why? What have we done as a society to make almost everyone not like themselves? And how, as parents, do we keep passing female body shame on to the next generation?

We, mother and daughter, are completely opposite in our self-mirror-monologues; one avoids looking at herself naked in the mirror while the other loves and thrives on it. We each experienced different dressing room talk with our mothers and received opposing messages about the validity of feeling beautiful.

Sheryl: Shopping with Mom was for the most part a lot of fun but did have its moments. My mom and I loved to shop for clothes, yet the dressing room talk I often heard was related to clothes that she felt were not flattering or appropriate for my body. When I was young, she would say things like, "The dress is too short and shows your big thighs, the horizontal stripes and wide belt make you look short and fat, and the neckline is too low and revealing and makes you look slutty." Even as I matured into adulthood I heard, "The sleeveless shirts make your arms look chubby, the prints are too busy and loud for your height, and the spaghetti straps are too thin and the bra straps stick out." My mom probably meant well and was trying to give me positive feedback on clothes she felt did not look good on me. Yet my interpretation of these comments was that something was wrong with my body.

One of the main sources of our "schlopping conflicts" revolved around the difference in what was appropriate for our body shapes and age. My mother had a perfect, slender body and could walk into any store, try on clothes, and almost everything fit, without the need for alterations. I, on the other hand, had a very different body shape. I began to develop rather early and reached my adult height of four feet nine when I was twelve years old. I always felt I was "overweight, a little on the chubby side," because my body just wasn't like most of my peers. I was told by doctors that according to the weight and height growth charts at that time I was a little overweight, and my mom used to reinforce this message by frequently telling me to "lose a few pounds." As a result, my perception of my body from a rather young age was that I was short and fat. Yet, in actuality, this perception may have been due to my short stature and muscular build. Looking back at photographs from that time, I now realize that the feeling of being overweight, fat, or chubby resulted more from my own self-image than from reality.

Mom and I would go into the dressing room with dozens of items for me, and I would be lucky if one outfit almost fit. Nothing ever fit perfectly and everything required extensive alterations, such as shortening the hem, shortening the sleeves, or adjusting the length of the straps. Finding that one item that "almost" fit was excruciating at times. Trying on so many clothes that did not fit my body shape and hearing the negative comments from Mom in the dressing room influenced my self-image and self-mirror-monologue in a negative way.

Gommie and my mom always emphasized the concept of dressing properly, appropriately, and stylishly. Although our style was neither high-end fashion nor haute couture, there was always the message that clothes, accessories, and even underwear had to match. As Gommie always said, "If, God forbid, something happens and you get into an accident and end up in the hospital, you don't want to be caught by the doctors or nurses with undergarments that aren't color coordinated." Even when she was eighty-seven years old and took a fall that led to her move to a nursing home, she was happy to let us know she had matching underwear and pantaloons on her arrival at the Emergency Room.

At school we had strict dress codes and were not allowed to wear pants or jeans but had to wear skirts and blouses or dresses. The predominant style at that time included shirtwaist dresses with a distinct and small fitted waistline, and for someone with a very short torso who is also short waisted that style was always challenging. As a result, from the age of thirteen I began sewing my own clothes and learned how to do all the alterations on store-bought clothes. I always loved clothes and accessories and made sure that everything matched, including bows and ribbons for my hair and laces for my shoes.

From a very early age, I never really saw myself as pretty. I was just the "short cute one" who never really looked as beautiful as other girls. I had dark hair and dark brown-green eyes, was very short, and had a body that was more muscular than the slim body that all girls then dreamed of. There were always the girls around me, in school, in scouts, in my youth group, who were more beautiful; the ones all the guys drooled over, the ones who had lists of boyfriends knocking at their doors. And then there was me! At least that is what I thought about me, back then growing up, and my personality took shape in this image.

Sometimes we remember and seem to hold on to the things that were said so many years ago. It might be a comment, bits and pieces of a conversation, or something in passing, perhaps a compliment or a criticism; yet what we think we heard becomes embedded in our memory and plays over and over again in our mind for years to come. An incident that happened at my brother's Bar Mitzvah remained with me for decades and shaped my self-esteem and body image. It was December 1961, and I was already a budding, physically maturing ten-and-a-half-year-old preadolescent. I remember shopping for the occasion and having to find several outfits for Friday night service at the synagogue, for Shabbat morning services, the evening party, and Sunday brunch. There were always conflicts, even back then, about what was appropriate to wear or not to wear, especially for special events.

My first cousin Lisa is three years older than me and from an early age started to do things that my parents did not approve of. Part of the dress code for school also included dress and skirt length, no more than seven inches above the knee, and hair teased less than two inches above your head. Lisa teased her hair and wore short dresses with low-cut, revealing necklines, heavy makeup, and high heels: all the signs of a promiscuous teenager according to my parents. I never could understand why the emphasis was on the way Lisa dressed rather than on the facts that she was intelligent and an avid reader and a loving and caring cousin. We often spent time together at our grandparents' home in the summer and holidays, and trips to the local library, at her request, were a daily event when we were together.

As a result, I was always dressed so that it would be clear that I was just a little girl, and the dresses that I got for Sam's Bar Mitzvah were picked to show my "little girliness." We looked for those special outfits that Mom and I thought made me look pretty and cute, and we were both excited when we found a few things that also fit me well. Those feelings of happiness, of finding the right dress and having Mom compliment me and tell me how beautiful I looked, in the dressing room in front of the mirror, were filled with the anticipation of the occasion.

All the family, including grandparents and other relatives, gathered at our house to get dressed up for the events. All of us women slipped into our dresses, styled our hair, applied makeup, and put on our fancy jewelry to make ourselves look as beautiful as possible. We all complimented one another and felt like a million dollars as we gazed into the mirrors before leaving the house.

I vividly remember having lots of people all weekend long telling me how pretty, beautiful, and cute I looked at the events. It was great for a young girl to get so many compliments from others, especially when I saw myself as never as pretty as my friends and a rather dowdy little girl. At some point after hearing so many compliments, I recall going up to one of my relatives and saying, "Aren't I pretty?" Mom overheard me and rather emphatically said, "Don't ever say those things; you should not tell others that you are pretty." My interpretation of what I heard, and what I remembered for many years to follow, was that you should never be vain about your looks and should not let others think that you think that you are beautiful.

It was a very mixed message. On the one hand, it was ok to feel beautiful in the dressing room when we found the perfect dress or when we all got dressed up for the occasion. But once we stepped out of the house, it was no longer appropriate to think of ourselves as beautiful. The message I remembered and held on to for many years was that one should never have positive feelings about oneself; one should be modest and not be vain. The message was also that if you think of yourself as beautiful, smart, and successful, you are a conceited, self-centered person. It was as if you were supposed to leave those confident feelings in front of the mirror and not show them outside the dressing room.

When we think of a memory of something someone has said, we remember the words and our interpretation of the message, which may not have been the intent behind those words. One of the messages I heard from Mom was that I should not think of myself as pretty; however, her intent was that I should not feel vain about my looks in front of other people. When Mom criticized the clothes on my body in the dressing room, she did not intend to make me feel that something was wrong with my body or that I was not beautiful; rather, she meant to give me helpful tips in the decision-making process.

Yael: My mom did everything perfectly. For me, going schlopping with my mom meant I was showered with compliments and was told how beautiful my body looked and how the clothes looked great on me. After going through all the racks and hearing my mom say numerous times, "This would look beautiful on you. Why don't you try it on?" we would go into the dressing room with dozens of items, and I would look forward to seeing myself in the mirror and hearing her praises.

Her dressing room comments are always positive about my body and any negative comments are about the clothes. For example, my mom always says, "That looks beautiful on *you*." To me, that always meant that the garment was not beautiful until I slipped my body into it and gave it "myself." When a dress was not flattering, she would feel the dress between her fingers and say, "Those hems are not even. They did a bad sewing job; let's find something nicer made." To me this meant the dress was lousy, and so even my own beauty could not make the dress look beautiful.

Since I was young, I've been able to look at myself naked and thrive; I have always thought I was the most beautiful woman in the world. I would compare and contrast myself as a human being to others and always in my mind felt that there was something pretty and special about me. Even if I looked at models in the media, I would think that there is at least one part of my body that was prettier. Not that I was perfect—I started to go gray at the age of sixteen and had severe acne—so I could have obsessed about my so-called flaws and not like my reflection in the mirror. But I did not. I truly believe that the way my mom constantly complimented me, especially in the dressing room, while she and I looked at me in the mirror, boosted my ego and wired my brain to have positive thoughts about my body and to have a positive self-image and self-mirror-monologue.

I remember when we went shopping when I was young and sales people would say, "That looks so beautiful on you!" and my response "Everything looks beautiful on me!" would shock them. Often, I thought I was vain because throughout my life I could always look in the mirror and say to myself, "Wow, you are gorgeous." I felt that because I was socially attractive and skinny and had nice boobs and a pretty face, it was wrong of me to think that I was pretty. I felt that if only I had a so-called flaw, I would not be considered vain but rather a woman with high self-esteem. But that was not true. I *could* have obsessed about anything and everything I saw in the mirror or the flaws other people might have thought I had, but I did not.

When I was twenty-four years old, right before my wedding, I finally gained five extra pounds and witnessed my body changing. I was always very skinny, probably due to dancing ballet every day for years and perhaps good metabolism. For the first time in my life, I could pinch a little tiny piece of skin and fat from my stomach and could no longer wrap my index finger and thumb around my arm. I knew I had gained some weight but it wasn't until I visited my parents and stepped on a scale that I knew how much. It was at that moment when I saw the five extra pounds registering on the scale that I understood how people can obsess about their fluctuating weight all their life. Although my weight had changed, I still thought of myself as beautiful and loved my new reflection. At that time, I made a conscious decision to feel beautiful about my body no matter what number labels got attached to it.

Today, in my mid-thirties, after several illnesses, two pregnancies during which my breasts inflated to a DDD cup, and breastfeeding my children, my body has finally really changed. However, I refuse to look at my body as being anything less than perfect. I look now at my naked reflection and see a beautiful, womanly body that gave life to and fed human beings. And although I can find many more "flaws" than I used to—scars, fat, sagging breasts, dry skin, and wrinkles—every time I look in the mirror my self-mirror-monologue is wired to think positive thoughts and see the beauty in my body. My first instinct is to say to myself, "Hello, Beautiful." When negative thoughts surface, I think of my feelings when I was twenty-four years old and make a conscious decision not to criticize my body but instead to love it just the way it is.

Thinking of me as anything less than beautiful will take away a huge piece of the essence of who I am, and I am not willing to forego that at the young age of thirty-six. Thus, I was not vain when I was younger. I was just an empowered woman who loved herself and who, I hope, will continue loving herself no matter what.

It is the positive record that I heard all my life from my mom, especially in the dressing room, that will continue to replay in my mind. All I can hope now is that I will be as good to my children as my mom was to me and that I will raise empowered human beings with a positive self-image and self-mirror-monologue.

Dialogue between Sheryl and Yael, October 2011, while Yael is breastfeeding her daughter

Yael: Is this what you thought throughout your life, that you're not beautiful?

Sheryl: Yeah, in a lot of ways. Recently, when I was preparing a presentation on the results of my Ph.D. dissertation and I found a picture of me as an adolescent in a shirtwaist dress and white oxford shoes, it looked like I was just there, on the edge of puberty. I had no waist, no hips or breast: they all seemed to merge as one. At that time, I always felt heavy and fat, but looking back now, as a middle-aged woman, I can see I was anything but fat; there was just some preadolescence chubbiness. When I recently found my journals from when I was fifteen years old, I read that I weighed 110 pounds with the measurements of 36-26-36, and that year one of my New Year's resolutions was to lose weight. But feelings of never liking my body stayed with me for many years to come. In fact, in 1978, when I was twenty-seven years old and designing my macramé jewelry and had long flowing hair with a little bit of gray, my body had seemed to change for the better after having you two kids. I vividly remember going into the municipality building of Jerusalem to register for the annual arts and crafts fair and a stranger looked at me and said, "What a beautiful woman." That remark could have been considered harassment, but as a woman who had never thought of herself as beautiful, I was shocked that others thought I was attractive.

Yael: I feel Savta Evelyn grew up in the Disney *Snow White* generation, where the woman who wanted to be beautiful was vain and evil and the woman who was modest and helpful was the better woman. You, Mom, grew up in the 1960s and wanted to empower me so I would have a positive self-image. Yet still in our society I feel that if we think of ourselves as beautiful, and we are socially beautiful, we are thought to be vain. So when is it ok to think of yourself as beautiful?

Sheryl: I think that you should always think of yourself as beautiful. And especially on special occasions, like a prom, a valentine party, a sweet sixteen, and certainly a wedding, you are allowed to and should feel good about yourself. However, I am sure that many people, even on these very special days, still don't really like how they look and would like to "feel a little thinner," although you and I know that you don't feel thin or fat.

Yael: Do you remember when we went to JCPenney out in the Natick Mall, and it was prom time and a lot of mothers and daughters were shopping for prom dresses? As we were in the dressing room, we overheard in the next stall a mother telling her daughter, "Your thighs are too big and your shoulders are too wide for that dress." I could only imagine how that daughter felt at that moment and how it affected her body image. If I had been told that my arms looked fat in that dress, I would probably obsess about how my arms look every single time I put on an outfit.

Sheryl: Of course I remember that schlopping trip. It was to find a dress for the Passover Seder, and we had to shop in the junior department even though you were in your thirties because you had lost so much weight after your illness. Hearing those words and seeing your face made me shiver inside to think of the impact that words could make. The mother did not say it in a malicious tone and probably thought she was helping her daughter choose the best dress. However, hearing a stranger's dressing room talk only reconfirmed the importance of not judging one's body while looking in the mirror.

Yael: So, Mommy Dearest, why and how did you bring me up the way that you did? How did you know or learn to mother me that way, or was I really just so beautiful (laughing)?

Sheryl: That is an interesting question. Perhaps I was doing the things that I had wanted to be done to me and tried hard not to replay the record of what I had heard in my childhood. Instead, I tried to create a new melody, a new song, a new and different way of thinking and allowing you the ability to learn to care about yourself. So when I would encourage you, from a very young age, to look in the mirror and see yourself as you put on a new dress, I would be thrilled to tell you how beautiful you looked and always loved to see your smile, not only reacting to what you heard me say, but also reflecting what you must have been feeling on the inside. Perhaps those memories from childhood in the dressing room of clothes being too tight or having lines that made me look heavy were not what I wanted to pass on to you. Of course, from a very young age, you had a beautiful slender body and always looked amazing in anything and everything you put on. I have a very vivid memory of when you and I went into a very upscale store and I encouraged you to just try on clothes without any intention to buy, just to see what they looked like on you. There was a velvet dress—neither of us remembers the color: I remember black and red and you remember black and green—and the dress looked beautiful on you. This was also at a time when your body was beginning to develop and take on the shape of a young woman. So what could be more beautiful to a mother than seeing your daughter grow up and start to take on the shapes and curves of a woman. You actually had none at that time, but just the presence of you in that dress made me realize how quickly you were growing up.

Yael: What would have happened and what would you have done if I had looked the way you thought of yourself looking as you were growing up?

Sheryl: I like to think that I would have acted the same way, and I believe I actually did with your brother, Yotam. When he was in college, Yotam and I went on a schlopping trip to buy professional work attire, probably the first schlopping trip since he was a teenager. I realized how important it was to talk about the clothes and not his body shape. The two of us went to the men's department and took dozens of shirts, pants, and belts for him to try on in the dressing room. Since Yotam is built like me, rather on the short side, he has a similar challenge in that almost nothing fits his body and sleeves and pants are always too long. I felt such a sense of *déjà vu*, but this time I was not the one trying on clothes, I was the parent gazing at my son in the mirror in clothes that didn't fit him properly. I think it was the first time I realized how difficult it was for him, in the same way it is for me, to find clothes that fit. In the back of my mind, I even thought that perhaps we should try clothes from the boy's department, but kept those thoughts to myself: How can I tell my twenty-year-old son to try on kid's clothes! I kept going back and forth to the racks of clothes, in the same way I always did with you, to bring different sizes and different colors. He finally found a few shirts that fit well and several pairs of pants, but of course all the slacks needed alterations and to be shortened in the hem. The whole time, I kept telling him how handsome he looks and when the clothes were too big, which they often were, we just kept looking until we found something that was a good fit.

Schlopping Tips

- Flatter yourself and your child at least once a day, especially in the dressing room or while gazing in the mirror.
- Always focus on the positive aspects of your body or your child's body. Any negative comments should be about the garment, not the body.
- Do not criticize yourself while gazing in the mirror; your child will imitate you.
- Resist the urge of giving "helpful tips" about what fits your child's body shape in the dressing room or in front of the mirror.
- Body shape conversations should take place privately while looking at other people, such as when comparing two celebrities wearing the same outfit.
- You can always change the record by going schlopping and having a positive dressing room talk, even with grown children.
- Those who have grandchildren have a responsibility to make sure that a positive record will be passed on.

4. Good-Fat Bad-Skinny: The Battle of the Sizes

**"2, 4, 6, 8, 10;
I can fit in that dress again."**

MANY TIMES, WEIGHT LOSS OCCURS because a person wanted to lose weight: they dieted, exercised, and changed their daily routine. However, often people lose weight due to causes that may be known or unknown to them, including cancer or other illnesses, chemotherapy, depression, or hormonal imbalances such as an over active thyroid. So if we tell somebody that she looks fabulous because she lost weight, are we basically telling that person that she is much prettier as a sick woman than as a healthy woman?

Some of us have experienced sudden weight loss and people's reaction is, "You look so good. You lost so much weight!" So what does this mean? Does it mean that we didn't look good before? Does it mean that if we gain weight again we won't look good? Rarely will a person come up to you and say, "You look so good. You put on a few pounds!" Sometimes we gain weight because we are happy, or went on a fabulous vacation, or we got over an illness. And often it is because we are feeding another human being and need all the energy we can get. So why don't people congratulate us on that?

Yael: Often, an illness or treatment changes our bodies, which can affect our personal self-image. We might look in the mirror and cry or look at old pictures of ourselves and wonder if we will ever look the same way again. For me, it manifested in not wanting to shop, ever!

Before I turned thirty years old, I was diagnosed with stage four endometriosis. I was the worst case my doctor, an endometriosis specialist in Boston, has seen in his entire thirty-five-year career. At least I was best in being the worst! Endometriosis, or, as I call it endo, occurs when the tissue that lines the uterus grows outside of the uterus on other organs of the body. One theory is that the menstrual blood does not regularly flow out of the body but rather stays inside the body and becomes scar tissue.

When I was young, my periods were very heavy, long, and painful. My mom told me what her mom told her: "After you get pregnant and have babies, it will be much better." I remember often when I was menstruating I could not even stand straight. In my mid-twenties, it changed: the flow of the blood became light yet lasted for almost two weeks and the color became dark brown and smelled horrible and I used to say it was the smell of death. Today I know it was because much of the blood did not come out of the body and the blood that did come out was old with little oxygen. The doctor I had then said it was a normal side effect of birth control pills. And so, for more than eighteen years, from the time I began menstruating, I was walking around misdiagnosed.

In 2006, I moved to Boston and was trying to get pregnant for more than a year without success. I started to have very bad back pains, which I thought was muscle strain due to dancing ballet. At that time, I was always nauseous, had difficulty eating, and lost a tremendous amount of weight. Although I had been skinny all my life, and used to fit into sizes 2 and 4, I went down to a size 0 due to my illness and was actually proud of my skinny body.

Finally, I went to a new doctor who listened to me as I explained my symptoms, and he thought I might have endometriosis. He tapped my back and suspected a blockage in the kidney, which was confirmed by an ultrasound. My endo was so severe that the tissue blocked my ureter, the tube that goes from the kidney to the bladder, and I almost lost my left kidney. The blood tissue also accumulated next to my bowel, resulting in what feels like an iron fist pushing into my lower back every month during my period, causing excruciating pain. My doctor immediately called his urologist colleague and they both scheduled me for an operation within forty-eight hours. It was a Wednesday, and my operation would take place on Friday.

My doctor said it would be a simple laparoscopy procedure, in which they would go through the belly button and clean all the scar tissue from the endo out of the body. The urologist would open the blockage in the kidney with a stent at the same time. It was supposed to be an ambulatory procedure and I would go home the same day. My doctor was known as the best doctor for laparoscopy procedures and everyone in the hospital said I was in good hands. I remember the resident doctor coming to me before the surgery telling me, "If there is a doctor who can succeed in this operation, through a laparoscopy and not an open abdominal surgery, it's him." At that time, I did not even contemplate an abdominal surgery as an option.

And so I was rolled into the operating room with anxiety but a smile on my face thinking I would be home within hours and all this would be behind me. I was under anesthesia when my doctor could not perform the laparoscopy. He went out to the waiting room with a worried face and showed my husband, Asaf, and my parents a picture of a healthy uterus next to an image of my uterus, which was surrounded by scar tissue. He told them there was too much tissue blocking the area and he was unsuccessful in resolving the situation with laparoscopy alone. He asked permission to perform an open abdominal surgery, which ended up lasting more than five hours. Often I feel that I still remember the music that was played in the operating room.

I never in my wildest dreams had thought that that day would be the beginning of a long and grueling nine months during which I lived with tubes and stents inside and outside my body as well as underwent dozens of procedures to protect my kidney. After the surgery, the doctors told me I could not try to get pregnant for at least a year in order to give my body time to heal. They also said that my endo was so severe that I might never be able to become pregnant or have children of my own.

I left the hospital four days after my operation with a stent inside my ureter and an external tube outside my left kidney, which was connected to a bag that collected the urine. The first few weeks all I could think of was trying to regain my strength and whether I would ever be able to become pregnant. Walking became difficult, breathing was painful, and I couldn't shower unless my husband was with me to tape a plastic bag over the tube so it would not get wet. He also changed the bandage when necessary. Later, Asaf told me that one of his daily thoughts was whether the place in the bandage was dirty or contaminated. He took such good care of me that I never had an infection in that area.

I was a twenty-nine-year-old professional woman who couldn't even shower when she pleased and all I could think of was that I might never have babies. I felt that my world had collapsed: I felt that if I could not have babies, I was not a real woman. It was as if I was a beautiful peach on the outside but rotten on the inside. So much of my identity was being a sexual woman and now all I could think of was that I would not be able to function as a natural woman should.

My body also changed in one day. From having this beautiful, "perfect" body and flat stomach, I suddenly had a cross-shaped scar on my abdomen and I ballooned up from a size 2 to a size 8 in a matter of months. All my self-image was flushed down the toilet along with the urine from the bag. I was depressed in the present because I was petrified for the future and what it meant in terms of my own family. All my thoughts were: Will I ever be pregnant? Will I ever have a kid? Will I ever become a mom? I became depressed and moody and often took it out on my husband and parents.

And so, with a tube and bag hanging out of my kidney and feeling I was not a real woman, I stopped wanting to shop. Just the thought of going in the dressing room and looking at my "deformed" body and not finding anything that would fit because I had a tube sticking out of my body was too much to bear. And so the way I coped with it was to eliminate shopping. I was working from home at that time and thus was able to just wear sweat pants or one of five pairs of pajamas my mom had bought me after the surgery. I was very depressed and self-conscious and seldom wanted to get dressed and make myself look pretty. Those pajamas were my professional attire for nine months.

A few months into the recovery, I needed to go to a graduate school interview. All my old suits were too small and I had no choice but to buy something new. I sent my mom to buy some suits, because I did not want to go shopping, and as usual she came back with sizes 2 and 4. When I tried them on nothing fit; I couldn't even get my leg through the pants. And so I gathered all my courage and went to the stores, schlopping with my mom. I was used to trying on sizes 2 and 4 all my life, and although I knew they would be too small I couldn't resist trying on suits sizes 2 and 4. When I went into the dressing room and none of them fit, I felt the sadness come over me. I went back out and picked up a size 6, but still nothing fit. I needed to go up to sizes 8 and 10. The first garment that fit was a size 8, the second garment that fit was a size 10, and the third was a squeezed-into size 6. I still remember the happy feeling of fitting into a size 6. In the dressing room, my mom confessed that she knew I was a size 6 or 8 or even larger but still bought me the smaller sizes. Her aim was threefold: first, she felt that if she brought back sizes 6, 8, or 10, I would be extremely upset and maybe even fume like a teenage daughter; second, she wanted to encourage me to go shopping and get over the fear of shopping; and third, she understood that I would need to accept my new body on my own. She decided not to be the messenger but rather let the clothes provide the message to me. The other problem I had was to find a suit that would allow me to hang my urine bag on my leg so it would be concealed. I went to the interview wearing a nice gray suit, size 8, and a beautiful pink blouse. I felt pretty, professional, and comfortable that the bag was not seen.

Throughout this ordeal, I always felt I needed to hide my bag from the public. I mean, who wants to see a bag full of urine? But on Halloween, I decided I would turn my defect into an effect and "dressed up" as a sick person and had my bag hanging out. When kids came to trick or treat, I opened the door carrying my bag, jokingly saying, "Watch out or I will squirt this bag on you!" They all laughed and loved my "costume"; little did they know it was real.

After almost a year, the stents and tubes were removed from my body and the kidney was no longer in danger. I was told I could finally start trying to conceive; it was terrifying. I guess not trying to become pregnant due to medical issues had felt like a relief since I temporarily escaped from trying and failing. The joy of trying to start a new family was overshadowed by the fear of not being able to conceive. I had to put all those thoughts away and be optimistic that my body would do what it was supposed to do. But it was hard.

Two years after the surgery, I was folding the laundry that included the pajamas I had worn, day in and day out, as my professional attire during those long, difficult months. It was as though the smell of the tubes and bandages came back as well as the feelings I had during the recovery and the fear of not being able to become pregnant. At that moment, I did something I had never done before. I gathered all my clothes that reminded me of the surgery and threw all of them out. Obviously, while doing it, as it was me, I thought maybe I should just hold onto one item as a piece of memorabilia, but I quickly decided against it. Why should I leave a painful memory in my closet? I wanted a fresh start. Thus, all the old pajamas were put in the trash and I went shopping for new pajamas.

Several months later, I was the luckiest woman in the world and got pregnant with my son. Perhaps it was the "cleansing of the closet" that got rid of the old sick me so that I could make room for the new life that was growing inside me. I loved being pregnant, I loved my growing belly and growing body, I loved being heavy, and I loved every extra pound I put on as it was the sign of health and life. One of my favorite things was to sit down and feel the heavy presence of my body on the chair; it was great to have all that weight. I also wanted to flaunt my belly everywhere, including buying a bikini to show my growing bump. I took a picture every week in the same pose, picking up my T-shirt and looking at my growing belly. Nothing but happiness and joy was beaming in my eyes. This time shopping for bigger sizes was the best thing I could do; I felt the bigger the better. Two years later, I got pregnant again with a daughter and loved every minute of it as well.

Seven years down the road—after I was blessed with two smart, kind, beautiful, and healthy children, a boy and a girl, completed law school, and passed the bar exam—my kidney unfortunately got blocked again. This time I lost an enormous amount of weight and everyone said, "You look so good and skinny." I even was able to fit into my wedding dress from a decade before.

But the weight loss was due to sickness rather than a good, positive event. Again, I became a size 0 and was worried about what this meant. I had an important meeting I needed to attend, but nothing in my closet fit; everything was too big this time. After two pregnancies, my wardrobe consisted of size 6 and 8 clothes and nothing smaller, so I went schlopping with my mom. I grabbed the size 4, but it was too big; I grabbed the size 2, but it was too big too; I went to a size 0 that finally fit and felt sick to my stomach. I looked in the mirror and did not like what I saw; it felt as if the suit was just hanging on a body, without any type of personality and strength coming out of that body. I was looking for the curves, the boobs, the butt, the hips, but nothing was there. It was like the clothes were on a hanger, and I wished I was a larger size. The main thing that was missing in that skinny outfit was life and joy in the eyes. My eyes looked sick, and once they look sick, no out-fit, no matter how big or small, will make me look beautiful.

I remember having a conversation a few months later with Asaf about my changing body and sexuality. He asked me what I now thought was the sexiest part of my body. After taking a few seconds, skimming all of my body parts from top to bottom and thinking about when I was the sexiest, I said, "My eyes." He looked at me, laughed, and said, "I didn't expect you of all people to say that, but you are completely right. It is, and always was, your confidence that beamed through your eyes that made you the sexiest woman in the room. Obviously, your perfect body and beautiful face helped, but that was not what made you amazing."

Our bodies not only change throughout the years but they also change within every second of every day. We breathe, eat, talk, digest, poop, and sweat and all those functions require a contrasting and extracting effect. When we inhale we expand and when we exhale we compress; when we eat we blow up and when we poop we go down; when we ovulate we grow and when the blood comes out we shrink. As a living organism, we fluctuate all the time.

Being beautiful is not about what you wear, the size of your clothes, or even how you look in them. It is about how you carry yourself and about your confidence, intelligence, compassion, and health, all of which reflect in your eyes.

Sheryl: Unlike Yael, who stopped shopping after her illness, for me shopping was the reconfirmation of life after I was diagnosed with breast cancer at the age of forty-three. My way of coping was to return to normalcy as soon as possible. I went back to work less than two weeks post-surgery and returned to my morning swimming routine as soon as the stitches and staples were removed. It took me several weeks to want to shop again; clothes just didn't seem to fit the same. My small right boob had become even smaller and I was self-conscious about my lopsidedness, so trying on clothes was not easy in the beginning. Clothes hung differently on that side, sleeves were too long, tight blouses accentuated the difference in size, and v-necklines were too revealing, showing the dot tattoos that had been strategically placed on my chest to "mark the spot" for radiation treatments.

When I tried on clothes, if I went alone, I always asked the salesperson if everything looked ok, because I knew that one side "hung longer" than the other. Only after they said, "It looks great!" and gave me more positive feedback would I say, with a laugh and a chuckle, that I only have half a breast and just wanted to make sure that it's not too conspicuous.

While undergoing my chemotherapy treatments, I went into early-onset menopause, a very common side effect. So in the same month, I went from menstrual cramps to hot flashes overnight. As a result, I gained a lot of weight and most of the clothes that hung in my closet no longer fit properly; I ballooned from a size 8-10 to a 12-14. The additional fifteen to twenty pounds on my short frame and the new menopausal body made me feel extremely self-conscious, and the only way to continue to look good and feel better was to hide the bulges under baggy clothes, oversized blouses, or sweaters and leggings. The only pants that fit over my rounded belly were those with a stretch elastic waist like old ladies wore.

The type of treatments I received did not cause total baldness, but my hair thinned out and started to fall out in large clumps, and the only solution to stop the shedding was to cut it very short, almost Twiggy style. At that time, I never wore any kind of makeup and certainly not lipstick. However, with my short hair and looking rather pale from the treatments, I added both to my everyday dress routine. So here I was, with a new hairstyle and a made-up face for the first time in my life. I looked better than before, and everywhere I went, people would say, "Sheryl, you look so good!" The irony was that even though I had gained so much weight and was rather plump for the first time in my life, I received so many compliments because people saw my radiant face and sparkling eyes, which somehow overshadowed the roundness of my body.

For several days following each chemo treatment, I was very fatigued. Yet, as soon as I started to feel better, the first thing I wanted to do was to go shopping. It didn't matter what it was, something big or something small, but it was always something just for me to feel alive and to do the thing that I always loved to do, to shop. I usually took my schlopping buddy Barbara with me to buy new jewelry, new clothes, and new shoes. When there were special occasions such as a wedding or a graduation ceremony, I would buy an entire new outfit from tip to toe, and even splurge on an expensive leather bag to match the new shoes. It was all about making me feel better and shopping was a way that I pampered myself, which helped me through the journey to recovery. During one of my schlopping sprees to the big city of Tel Aviv, which I did often at that time, I ran into someone I had not seen in several years, since her divorce. She looked at me and said, "You look great. Did you recently get divorced as well?" I answered, "No, it's just the glow from radiation."

I dealt with the extra weight by buying clothes that fit my new changing body. I just accepted the changes that were taking place because it was a sign to me of getting well. I actually felt that the additional weight was good for me, because several days after each chemo treatment I was unable to eat and lost so much fluid due to side effects of the medications that I believed I needed the extra baggage to maintain my strength. I guess I succeeded in finding a way to balance the weight gain and still look and feel good. This was one of the only times in my life that I was not frustrated by weight gain because I knew that the weight gain was a side effect of the treatments and that my body was overcoming the illness.

Several years later, I started to speak publicly about my cancer experience. I began the presentation by showing several pictures taken pre- and post-treatment in order to emphasize the changes of my body. At the end of treatments, I had very short, thin, white hair and a very puffy, fat, and full face, yet people in the audience always felt uncomfortable commenting on these aspects of my appearance. But I can imagine that had I lost the same amount of weight, people would probably have complimented me on the weight loss.

At these public speaking engagements, I also emphasized the importance and legitimization of pampering oneself through shopping. Recently, I heard that in online forums women now talk about the importance of "retail therapy" while undergoing cancer treatments. Last month at my annual checkup, my breast cancer oncologist told me about a patient of hers who bought new earrings after each chemo treatment. In 1994, there was not yet widespread internet service and retail therapy had not entered the mainstream nomenclature, yet somehow I knew that shopping was my savior.

Five years later, after Breast Cancer 1, I lost a tremendous amount of weight in a very short time and was not feeling well. Most everyone I knew said, "You look so great—you've lost so much weight." However, only one person, who knew of my cancer history, said, "You've lost so much weight. Are you feeling ok?" Here I was fatigued, depressed, and feeling like a sick person, yet everybody including myself congratulated me on my weight loss. After nine months of undergoing numerous tests and dozens of doctors' visits to cardiologists, neurologists, hematologists, rheumatologists, and gynecologists, I was finally diagnosed with hyperthyroidism—an overactive thyroid, which was the reason for the sudden weight loss. Several months later, I was able to balance it with medication and as I started feeling better I gained weight and returned to my healthy, energetic self. Even today when I have an unusual weight shift and people say how good I look, it is usually because my thyroid is imbalanced. I wish people today would congratulate me when I gain weight as opposed to only when I lose weight.

Dialogue between Sheryl and Yael, October 2011, Halloween time

Sheryl: The body image we develop from a very young age seems to be embedded in our memory even if there are substantial changes in our body. I always thought of myself as a heavy person, and even now when I look in the mirror and see a thin woman with curves, it is still difficult for me to see an attractive body. Only when others look at me and compliment me do I think positively about myself. But you, Yael, always thought of yourself as thin with a beautiful body no matter how your body changes. I look at you now as a beautiful woman with the curves a seven-week-post-partum woman should have.

Yael: The way you say it, Mom, is not complimentary at all, just the opposite. It makes me feel overweight and unattractive. You are not saying that I am attractive, but rather you are saying that under the circumstances I am attractive.

Sheryl: I am laughing because I worry more when I see women who in a very short time are proud of the fact that they have removed all of their "pregnancy baggage." Whereas I look at you and I am happy to see that you are happy and satisfied with who you are and with your body at this point and loving what your body is doing for you and your baby. This takes me back to when a neighbor said to me, only three months after you were born, "Oh, you are still so fat!" and another woman in the neighborhood said to her, "Leave her alone. She just gave birth a few months ago." I like the fact that it is not a concern for you. You always were a person who accepted your body despite the difficult times you went through and I am very happy that you still like to look at yourself both naked and dressed and that it has not turned into an obsession of losing weight after pregnancy. I think you look beautiful and I like the roundness of your body.

Yael: So what you are saying is I am round, round like a ball?

Sheryl: I am saying you have curves like a woman. I've been thinking about that while going through my wedding album. I always dreamed of a garden wedding, wearing my mother's dress that had been designed for her in 1947. Although I was a bit shorter, I assumed that I would also be able to fit into the dress, even though I had never actually seen it, since it was packed away in a closet in Columbus, Texas. It was 1972 when I got married, and my parents had just celebrated their twenty-fifth anniversary, and before Mom sent over the wedding dress with friends to Israel, she put it on and posed for pictures. Yes, she looked radiant and beautiful, maybe even more than when she was married at the age of twenty. However, in retrospect, should we, after twenty-five years and in our forties, look like we are in our twenties? For my mom, it was really important. For many years, I was convinced that my mother had eating issues that affected her weight and body image.

Yael: What did you think she was?

Sheryl: Although back then anorexia was not a commonly known disease among young women, I was always suspicious that she might have had some eating issues when she was growing up. Her mother had a fuller body, and in my mother's eyes she was fat and she always said, "I don't want to be as fat as Gommie." Mom needed to finish all of her food on her plate in order to get dessert and once told me that she used to hold her food in her mouth and then spit it out as a way of not eating. From as long ago as I can remember, Mom always had a stunning body, yet there was an overtone of worry about not gaining weight and remaining thin. Under stress, she would lose her appetite and not want to eat, while I on the other hand can't stop *noshing*. When we had our twenty-fifth wedding anniversary party and I took out my wedding dress from the storage suitcase in the closet to put on display in the living room, I was well over the 95 pounds I weighed when I was married—closer to 130—and felt happy that my body was no longer the way it was when I was twenty-one. I was actually happy that I no longer could fit into the dress.

Yael: You felt your body was healthy?

Sheryl: Yes, it was two years after Breast Cancer 1 and I still had a larger body than today. The idea of my chubbiness and the battles over being a few pounds overweight have continued with me, but subsided in recent years. Recently, I switched out the winter and summer clothes, and when I put on my size 10 pants, they looked better on me than the size 12, and that made me happy. And yet, for some reason, I cannot part with the numerous pairs of pants in size 12 and 14. Perhaps I fear that one day I will gain the weight back and need to "shop in my closet" for those larger size pants.

Yael: (Laughing) So even with all your psychological blah-blah, we are both still slaves to the thin and beautiful. You feel good because you fit into a smaller size.

Sheryl: I am planning to go in a couple of weeks to a Halloween party, a benefit for my breast cancer rowing team, We Can Row, and I decided a couple of nights ago, perhaps after our recent schlopping trip, that I am going to go as a belly dancer and need to find the appropriate costume. This is a real challenge for me since such a costume would reveal both the belly as well as the boob. In fact when I told a teammate of mine what I was planning and asked her if she wanted to join me, she declined, stating that she has too many body image issues to go in such a revealing costume.

Yael: So I am going to say something really, really harsh. From your face, it seems that you feel sorry for her that she has body issues and she can't do what you can do. Am I right, Mom?

Sheryl: Yes. She is only forty years old and has gone through numerous breast cancer surgeries over the last five years, and I think that age has a lot to do with that. It's interesting, since I am not sure that I would want this level of exposure in other venues. However, that party will be with close friends of mine who have all gone through breast cancer. I went to a costume store and tried on several belly dancer outfits and felt they revealed too many bulges, thus decided not to go as a belly dancer. I went to the storage unit to find the costume box, which has various items I have kept over the years, including several of my favorite dresses that I sewed in the 1960s, a maxi dress, a jumper with a faux-leather top and plaid skirt, various hats and gloves from Gommie's closet, Indian tie-dye skirts and hand-embroidered shirts from the 1980s, and the purple-pink cocktail dress I bought in 1982 for my macramé art show opening at the Artery in Davis, California. I remember buying that dress. It was the first time I bought such a fancy dress, a cocktail dress, with a low-cut v-neck, spaghetti straps, and a fitted waistline design. When I bought it, almost thirty years ago, I had been working out daily in a gym for several months and my body had taken on a different shape and I felt I was able to wear such a dress.

The last time I wore that dress was in 2000 for Purim, for a costume party, the year that I lost an enormous amount of weight due to my hyperthyroid problem and was able to fit into clothes that I had not worn in many years. I went from a size 14 to a size 10 in a matter of months and in the beginning was actually very happy that I had lost so much weight. Now in 2011, I brought these items home and started trying them on. The turquoise harem pants that I bought in 1985, a year after Dad passed away, that I so loved back then, were too small, as was everything else. Then I put on the purple-pink cocktail dress and it actually fit. There was only one small exception: when I put it over my chest while wearing my prosthetic boob, it was too tight. So I put the dress on boob-less and went out to show your dad. His reaction was, "It looks great, but shows the scar," which in fact it did. So I tried tying a bright yellow feather boa in different ways that would conceal the scar until I realized that the beauty of the dress was the low cut revealing neckline. My next thought was perhaps to get a temporary tattoo to put over the scar.

Yael: Why a tattoo?

Sheryl: I guess my first reaction is that I would like to go with a revealing scar. After all, this is a benefit for our breast cancer team and it is October, Breast Cancer Awareness Month, and the dress is purple-pink, which all seem to make a statement. The question was, do I reveal a scar and boob-less chest in public this way? I have never really shown my naked boob-less chest in public. In fact, I have a whole self-monologue about where I go without a boob and still feel comfortable. I would not think twice about not wearing my boob for rowing with We Can Row or paddling with the Wellness Warriors, cancer wellness teams. However, I always wear the boob when I go rowing in other groups or to races in public. For me, the cancer groups are my private space whereas the other situations are more public.

Yael: Well, what is interesting about scars is sometimes I feel that on men they are a sign of heroism, achievements, or accomplishment, whereas on women they are a source of embarrassment. After my operation, I had a cross-shaped scar on my belly, moved to Carson City, Nevada, and needed to go shopping for a new bathing suit. All my life, I had only worn two-piece bathing suits, and while going through the racks I was contemplating whether I should buy a one-piece in order to conceal my scar. After two minutes of deliberating, I decided to continue with my tradition of two-piece bathing suits and showing the scar. I did not want this scar—now at my young age of thirty—to change the way I feel or make me shameful about my body. Yotam bought me a magnet that says, "Scars are tattoos with better stories." Now I think that you and I are different, because you always talked about wanting a tattoo on your scars, and I never thought about changing or concealing my scar. But I do have to go back and say that your face was beaming and your eyes were glowing when you said that you fit into the dress that you bought thirty years ago. So maybe that judgment on your mom was not fair or maybe it was that you could not fit into your wedding dress twenty-five years later. I definitely will not be able to fit into my wedding dress that I wore ten years ago—no way.

But I did fit in that dress again, two years later, following another kidney blockage.

Schlopping Tips

- Don't be a slave to the size numbers; buy the size that you feel good in.
- Losing weight is not always good, and gaining weight is not always bad.
- Fitting into old, smaller clothes may be a sign of diminishing health.
- The way you feel, the way you carry yourself, and the spark in your eyes is what makes you look beautiful, not the pounds on the scale or the size of the dress.
- Don't congratulate people just because they lose weight, and don't think badly of someone just because they gained weight.

5. Schlopping for the Boob-Less Bra

"Is that what will define my femininity?"

Sheryl: From as long ago as I can remember, my right breast was always quite a bit smaller than my left, and as a result I was extremely self-conscience from a very young age. I thought I was the only one with lopsided boobs until I met my good friend Maris when I was about twenty years old and realized I was not an anomaly. That was not the only reason I never let a guy in high school get past first base, but that was certainly part of it. Back then in the 1960s, there were the "good girls" and the "bad girls." I was one of the good girls, and too much physical contact was not what one did among my cohort of high school nerds, who sat around discussing philosophical and political issues and how to make the world a better place. Although making out was part of my growing-up experience, petting and sex were not high school adventures of mine. Sure, we made out, but kissing was about as far as it went. The first time "it" happened, letting a guy touch my breast, was after I graduated high school. One of my closest friends, who many years later came out of the closet and has since lived as a gay man, had just finished a year of college. He convinced me that touching breasts was just part of the growing up experience, so I took the plunge. Most of my embarrassment was due to the lopsidedness of my boobs, but, to my utter surprise, he didn't even notice.

I have never liked the constraints of wearing a bra, and when you have such lopsided boobs, bras never fit. Often, I preferred just to not wear anything, fitting in well with the atmosphere of the 1960s. Of course, during pregnancies and breastfeeding I did wear the contraption. But after the birth of my daughter, Yael, my boobs just shrank. In fact, there were years when I didn't even own one, partly due to the discomfort of not being able to find one that fit and partly because I just didn't like to wear a bra.

In 1982, I began teaching English to adults and felt uncomfortable and a little embarrassed about having my bra-less boobs jiggling around and went back to wearing bras on a more regular basis. From as long ago as I can remember, buying bras was always a very time-consuming, frustrating, and stressful event. It's not easy—actually it's almost impossible—

to find a bra that fits when on one side you are a C cup and on the other a B cup. I would try on dozens of bras and be lucky if I found even just one or two styles that fit. Eventually, I found one style, Victoria's Secret "Emma," an underwire, front-closing C cup with soft nylon that would shape to the boobs. That was the only style I bought for over ten years. For years those worked and I could even buy a C cup and the stretch material of the cup of the bra would mold itself around the smaller, right, size-B boob.

In 1994, at the age of forty-three, I went in for a routine breast examination and a lump was found in my right breast, the small one, the B cup. I was diagnosed with stage 1 invasive ductal carcinoma breast cancer in my right breast, and the recommendation was to have a lumpectomy, a procedure that removed the lump and the surrounding breast tissue, followed by chemotherapy and radiation. Needless to say, my B cup shrunk to an A cup, while my C cup remained the same, making me even more lopsided than before. Yael always used to joke, "Hey, Mom, if it had only happened on the big side, it would have evened out your boobs!"

I will always remember that right after the surgery, after losing half of my small breast, and the removal of eleven lymph nodes, it was almost impossible to wear a bra, and especially an underwire bra, because the underwire would just hit the site of the incision, causing additional pain and irritation. No one back then told me about the aftereffects of a lumpectomy: that not only would I lose half of my boob, but that it would look deformed for several months. The little skin that was left seemed to just point out in the strangest directions, and I couldn't put on any bras that I owned.

I went alone to the local mall to find something that would work. The idea of taking Yael, who was a teenager at the time, was not something that even came to mind. She may have felt the lump the night before I went into surgery, but I don't recall if she even saw my naked lopsided, surgically deformed boobs at that time. I was lucky to find a few nice stretch exercise bras, size medium without designated cup size, that just worked. The stretch material kept the left side C upright and fit softly and smoothly over the still healing surgical site and sensitive tissue of the A cup right side.

Several months after my surgery, after the uncomfortable sensation subsided, I was able to go back to my one-and-only Victoria's Secret "Emma." However, at some point in the 1990s, this style was discontinued, and to my chagrin I had to start my search again for the not-so-perfect fit of a new style. Again Victoria's Secret came to the rescue, since they began making an all-cotton, underwire bra. This time, however, a C cup did not work because it puckered too much on my A cup boob and, therefore, I made a strategic decision to average them out between the C and the A and bought a 36 B. It fit the small right boob with minimal puckering and the big left boob was squashed and popped out a little. My poor C cup boob needed to be compressed in a B cup bra for more than a decade.

Sometime in 2007, when I was ordering new bras, I was devastated to discover that the cotton bra, the only one I had worn for more than a decade, was being discontinued. Therefore, I ordered "everything" that Victoria's Secret had in stock, almost two dozen, in all colors, 36 B, and figured they would last a lifetime if I took out just a few new ones each year.

However, a year later, in 2008, at the age of fifty-seven, small microscopic calcifications were found in the right breast again, the A cup, during my routine mammogram. I was diagnosed with DCIS, ductal carcinoma in situ, which is the presence of abnormal cells inside the milk duct. Since I previously had undergone a lumpectomy and radiation in that breast, the only surgical option I had was to have a mastectomy, which meant losing the breast completely. The question that occupied my mind was "to do or not to do," whether to have a reconstruction or not. Since so much breast tissue had already been removed in Breast Cancer 1 and since I had extra belly fat, the only reconstruction option was the TRAM, transverse rectus abdominis myocutaneous, in which tissue from the abdomen is transferred to the breast.

At that time, it was unknown whether or not I would need any follow-up treatment, such as chemotherapy; that would only be decided following surgery and after a review of the pathology reports. So here I was, a little older than the previous time, a little more aware of the consequences of cancer itself, and determined to make a decision that was best for me at that time. I want to note that I am not a carrier of either of the known BRCA genes for breast cancer. I therefore did not need to decide whether to undergo a bilateral mastectomy, which would have involved removal of the healthy left breast, which is prophylactic treatment if a woman carries those genes. This was not even discussed as an option or recommendation. So the only decision that I had to make was to do or not to do a reconstruction.

I took this decision very seriously and did extensive research on the benefits and risks of this procedure. During my research on how to make the best-informed decision, I felt as if I was implementing the model I developed several years prior for my Ph.D. dissertation on how women use different types of knowledge to learn about health issues. The model includes four types of knowledge: one, information you get from the medical field, which is called authoritative knowledge; two, information you experience yourself or gain from other people's experiences, which is called embodied knowledge; three, what procedures insurance would cover, which is called technical knowledge; and four, information passed on from your family and friends, which is called traditional knowledge.

I researched the surgeon online to better understand her medical background and expertise and looked online at the recommended surgical procedure and saw pictures of successful and unsuccessful reconstruction (authoritative knowledge); I reached out to several women who chose to have or not to have a reconstruction and asked them questions about their personal experiences (embodied knowledge); I called my insurance company to see what procedures it would cover (technical knowledge); I talked to my family and friends to get their opinion (traditional knowledge); and I kept a journal during this whole decision process. I had one week to make the decision and I vacillated between "to do or not to do" a reconstruction.

Excerpts from my journal during the decision-making process:

April 5, 2008—12:10 a.m.

Well I got the diagnosis today. It is carcinoma in situ and as the radiologist said, "It's not life threatening," which is very reassuring at least. Actually, the big dilemma is "to do a reconstruction or not to do a reconstruction, that is the question." I have decided to give myself more time to think about this. . . . I am not sure why the hesitation, after all shouldn't I be mourning the loss of my breast? But somehow I just don't seem to feel that it's really such an issue. It's just a piece of fat that hangs on my body, an appendix that has lost its sensation, its sensuality or aesthetics. It's always been smaller than the other one, and after the first breast cancer it just became "much, much smaller." I kind of laughed when the surgeon mentioned today that I would be a "perfect candidate" for reconstruction and that I would get a tummy tuck and my breasts would "be more symmetrical," so I asked, laughingly, "What, they aren't symmetric?" I just can't believe that this is the issue, to add the lump or not? I guess I need something to obsess about, so let this be it. . . . I have just wasted another half hour thinking about this and getting articles about my surgeon and I just found out that she is doing research on this topic. So am I just part of her research? Is this why she is pushing this so much? I assume. But I also have to decide that I am going to make a decision based on what I *want* and not what others think I want or need. I just don't understand why I think it doesn't matter to me. . . . I understand her agenda is to "give me information," but I also want all of the information. I feel like the women who are being pushed to breastfeed (how ironic that I think of this analogy) when they just don't want to, or the women who are pushed into knowing the sex of the baby before birth "because everyone wants to know." Maybe I really don't want to have a reconstruction, maybe it really doesn't matter to me. I appreciate that they are trying to give me all the information, but I also want to know about all of the adverse effects as well. What concerns me is how fast I will be able to get back to being myself after all this. Part of me just wants to do the surgery and get over it asap and see how I feel without anything. I want to find out what the implications are if I choose to just do that and then later on decide how to proceed. Part of me is the other side of vanity, that this is me and this is something that has happened and I would rather give the natural a try and then see about something else. I worry about waking up after surgery and having two very painful places that will need to recuperate and how that will affect me as well. I think that the sooner I can be back on my feet the better. I just can't believe that this is what is bothering me???? . . . I just want to be able to walk and swim as soon as possible, to get my body back to myself, and I am not 100% that having that extra skin from my belly will be the magic that will help me. . . . I also think about long term and what happens as my body changes, which is what it has done over the years and in the years to come, if I gain weight, I'll get larger breasts and if I lose weight, the breast shrinks. What will happen over the years if that does happen . . . is that what will define my femininity or me as a woman?

April 7, 2008—11:57 p.m.

Am I just in denial? Or perhaps I just haven't really accepted that I do have cancer. I have been doing everything to avoid the reality that I will lose a breast, laughing and joking about it, about cleavage, about everything else other than the fact that I do have cancer and for some reason I have had more energy, have been funnier than I have in a long time and even happier than I remember myself. . . . Or is it just that I am happy to have the kids here together with us, and just enjoying our time together as a family again, laughing and doing all the stupid things that we do. . . . After seeing all of those pictures of the operation and the scars and the bodies I am almost having second thoughts if I really want to go through all of that now. . . . Then you hear about so many people who aren't really happy, with problems, of drainage, of pain, of losing sensation, etc. . . . I feel that everyone is rushing me into this and I am just not sure that this is what I want to do. Is having fat on my breast really the most important thing for me at this point in my life? . . . I guess I do want to speak to others about it and see how they coped, but as I know, every case is different. . . . Do I honestly feel that not having a breast will be ok or will Sam not want to touch me or look at me with such a horrible scar? But that "breast" will only be a piece of flesh that has migrated from my belly to my breast.

April 8, 2008—9:40 a.m.

I am still undecided, but I have decided to get as much information about all aspects that I can, including reconstruction as well as not reconstruction. I also have made a decision that whatever decision I make I will not regret and will just have to accept and deal with and work with this. There will be no "I'm sorry I did this," or, "If only I had done something else," once I finally decide, then I will have to go with it.

April 9, 2008—7:17 a.m.

. . . I just keep thinking about what it will be like in the swimming pool, and I don't want to float with a prosthesis, but just want to be able to get into a pool and swim as soon as possible. Do I float (with falsies) or will I swim diagonally (without anything) or will it just be more natural?

April 10, 2008—12:08 a.m.

Well, I spoke with two women this evening, one a fifty-seven-year-old who had a mastectomy and did not do reconstruction. However, she also does not wear anything, just wears loose clothes and is fine with that. She said that she had no pain from the surgery. She had a friend who did a reconstruction and said that she was happy with it but it was six weeks of hell.

The other women had a mastectomy thirteen years ago at the age of thirty-five (had a kid at the age of forty-two), and she could not say enough good things about a reconstruction. She had friends who did not do it and they said they were really happy that they did not do it, but as soon as they got into their house, couldn't wait to take off their bra. She was very happy and this was done many years ago, when the techniques were much different. The most important thing she said was that it felt like her own skin; it was warm and felt good; when she gained weight, the breast also gained weight (that sounds creepy); and that when people look at her, "They can't tell the difference!" I guess that is important. Woman Number 1 said that it's hard to wear a T-shirt, you can just wear baggy clothes and it doesn't show, and Woman Number 2 said that you can wear the same clothes. The other important thing that she said was that there was more pain from the lymph nodes than from the stomach. This is all very encouraging. And when I hung up the phone I made my decision to do it. All in all, it's a good time, in between semesters, so I won't be too stressed, won't have much besides busy paper work at work . . . It just seems right to do now and not wait.

I see my surgeon tomorrow and the plastic surgeon (for a consultation) on Monday and will make a decision. I think I am now leaning (was this meant to be a pun?) toward reconstruction after getting a lot of information, etc. It just may be the best for me.

April 10, 2008—2:41 p.m.

I am back to where I was yesterday, undecided! I just spoke to a woman in her sixties who had a mastectomy and actually teaches water aerobics and is very happy with a prosthesis and gave me names of sites for bathing suits.

April 11, 2008—6:19 a.m.

Yael and I went to see the surgeon yesterday and first went to try on a prosthesis with the boob fitter. I decided that it would really be a good idea to actually see and feel what the prosthetic boob is like. She took me into a dressing room and handed me a boob that I put into the bra on the right side and voila, I had a regular size breast that matched the other side. In fact, she said that I could have been using this all along and I said that it didn't bother me, but once I put in that breast and made it the same size as the "me breast," I realized that it really looked nice and more than that, that it felt really good . . . When she asked me what my other options were and I told her the TRAM, she had a look on her that said a lot. She told me that she sees the women who are really in bad shape and has to help them get fitted, I guess after a reconstruction that doesn't work. She also said that there are reasons that your stomach muscles are in your stomach. I must have been inside about ten minutes wearing the boob and it really felt good, you kind of just forget about it. It also looked really nice—for the first time in my life I had a really nice right boob and the same size as the left!

I then went into the doctor to discuss the situation. The first thing we began speaking about was the reconstruction. She went on to show me on a scale where these operations are in terms of a lumpectomy and heart surgery. On a scale of 1 to 10, lumpectomy is 1, mastectomy is 3, and reconstruction is 7.

That was when I realized how serious the surgery actually was. We talked a little more about reconstruction and I started with my list of questions about the diagnosis and the surgery. . . . I kept thinking that I am not thirty, nor forty, and not even so close to fifty. Even though I only have three more years until I get there, it's really difficult to believe that I am actually closer to sixty! And all those things went into my decision-making process.

Sheryl: The final decision was based on four things: One, asking my surgeon where a reconstruction appears on a scale of severity and coming to understand it was closer to open-heart surgery; two, looking at pictures of the surgical procedures online and understanding the complexity of this surgery; three, hearing the boob-fitter talk about failed reconstructions and the loss of stomach muscles; and four, thinking of Yael and what she had gone through with her painful abdominal surgeries two years prior and understanding how incapacitated I might be following the surgery. I chose not to have a reconstruction, and my surgery was scheduled for April 28, 2008. Six days prior to the surgery, Yael and I went schlopping for bras.

Final Excerpt from Sheryl's Journal:

April 22, 2008—6:57 a.m.

I met Yael about 5 p.m., and we went to find a place to eat and found one near Macy's. . . . We then went to Macy's to look for clothes, saw nothing, and headed down to the bras and nightgowns, pajamas. . . . I decided that I wanted to try on other bras since I am now looking for a bra that will "fit the big one." As soon as I got undressed in front of Yael, who has not seen me naked in MANY, MANY years, she said, "Wow, you really are lopsided and the little one is really little." . . . Well, to say the least I was astounded and had the feeling that I was a 36 C and, boy, was I a 36 C!!!! I kept on trying and trying and Yael kept running back and forth to the racks, bringing different sizes, different colors, different styles, and making sure I had what was right. It was absolutely amazing when I started to try on the sexy ones! I have not wanted to go bra shopping in many, many years and part of this was because of the lopsided boobs I have so that I could NEVER find the bra that fit. . . . All of a sudden, when I realized that I had a nice bust—the big one looked really nice and when I put on a T-shirt—it looked amazing!!! It was so much fun, so fulfilling (not a pun intended!), to know that at least part of my body is still intact and beautiful and sexy and something that I will want to show off.

Sheryl: The schlopping trip with Yael for bras prior to my mastectomy surgery was such a good idea. It was both liberating and exciting to actually be able to buy bras in any style that would fit my C cup. Here I was, ready to lose a breast and for the first time in my life was preparing myself for symmetrical boobs. That trip reaffirmed my decision not to do a reconstruction.

The night before surgery I took pictures of my breasts, just to remember what they looked like, and it was only after looking at the pictures that I realized how lopsided I really was. After surgery and before I was fitted for a prosthesis, I put stuffing material into the pocket of a postmastectomy bra, put on a T-shirt, and went out to the living room to show Sam, Yotam, Yael, and Asaf my new breast. The reaction from all was, "You need more stuffing: you are still lopsided!" in a teasing, loving manner. Even when I went to purchase my first prosthesis, I opted for a size 7 instead of a size 8. I guess out of habit and after almost fifty years of being lopsided, it just feels best when my right boob is a little smaller.

For some women, reconstruction surgery is the right decision because it helps them continue their life after cancer. For me at that point in my life and at my age, it was not and I opted for a mastectomy only, without a reconstruction. I view these decisions as being very personal because each woman has her own circumstances and experiences and needs to make an informed decision based on her needs. Several months after the surgery, my surgeon and I worked on a concept paper that adapted the model of knowledge acquisition and applied it to the process of decision making following the diagnosis of breast cancer. This paper was published in 2011 in the *Breast Journal.*

After the mastectomy, all the Victoria's Secret 36 B bras no longer fit and I now needed 36 C. I called the company and explained the problem, that I had had a mastectomy, and they allowed me to return all the unopened bras, perhaps about fifteen of them. They sent me a gift card so I could now buy the size that would fit both of my boobs.

Five years later, while I was getting dressed, my grand-daughter, who was two at the time, entered the room and looked at my naked chest and touched the right, boob-less side and asked, "Where is your teat?" I explained, "I had a boo-boo, it was sick, and it needed to come off." She then asked, "Does it hurt?" I replied, "It used to, but not anymore." She then hugged me and very softly and gently clutched my left boob and looked into my eyes with joy and love.

Yael: I was a teenager when my mom got cancer the first time, and I probably did not handle it very well. My mom never wanted to scare us or to make us think that we might lose her, so she continuously joked about it and reassured us that every-thing was going to be fine. She acted like she would be able to overcome the cancer just like she overcame a regular cold. Often, I felt that nothing was wrong and everything would be ok and only got scared when I talked to my friends about it and saw their reaction.

I was a typical teenager and fought with my mom A LOT. Even when she got cancer and went through that ordeal, I continued my regular behavior: being mad at her if she cleaned my room without consent, as I felt she was invading my privacy; saying there was nothing to eat in the house and whatever was in the fridge was disgusting and so making her feel she needed to prepare food for me; and claiming over and over again that I was too busy with schoolwork, extracurricular activities, and friends so that I didn't have time for anything else.

I never went with her to the hospital to get treatments, and after her chemotherapy sessions I would often go to a friend's house to spend the night. She said that she preferred me out of the house so that I would not wake up when she went to the bathroom to vomit, but I wonder if that was really true. Often I look back at my behavior and think how selfish I was. How could I have continued life as if nothing was happening? Why didn't I take care of my mom in her time in need?

I remember that after she came home from her first chemotherapy treatment, I was complaining like a little brat that I had a party to go to the next day and had nothing to wear and I asked my mom if we could go schlopping. I knew she could not resist going schlopping no matter what her physical state was. So we drove to the local mall and went from store to store and after about forty-five minutes my mom said to me something that she had never said before: "Yael, hurry up and choose your clothes. I don't feel well." Little did I know she was nauseous and dizzy and miraculously was able to keep all her fluids in until we got home and she hit the bathroom. As I heard her puke her guts up I thought of three things: one, of my poor mom who was feeling so ill and fighting for her life; two, that I was so lucky to have such an unselfish mom who cared about me so much; and three, about the great dress we had bought and how beautiful I would look in it that night. It was as if my mom was the epitome of unselfishness and I was the epitome of selfishness.

Until today, the thing I regret the most is that one day, after my mom had ballooned up due to chemotherapy, I said, "Wow, Mom, you've gained so much weight. I would die if I was that fat!" Needless to say my mom was stunned and hurt. There is no excuse for my behavior, although my mom, being the great mom she is, always tells me that I dealt with her cancer the best way I knew how. I was petrified about losing my mom and my way of coping was to deny that anything wrong was happening. I guess also it is sometimes difficult as a teenager to consider somebody else's needs, especially your parents', and often we are so consumed by our own life that we can't consider others. Or maybe that was just my way of dealing with it: by continuing to live normally as if nothing had happened. After all, that was what my mom instilled in us—normalcy even in this state.

"Lucky" for me, I had a chance to redeem myself when she got cancer again. This time around, I was an adult, pre-motherhood, and I tried to help her as much as I could. We went schlopping for bras before and after surgery, I went with her to the boutique to try on her fake boob, and I sat in the waiting room in the hospital while she was undergoing surgery. But, even then, my mom continued to tell me not to worry, that she would be ok, and that my surgeries and procedures with endo a few years prior had been so much more severe, although they had not.

I remember looking at her little boob the night before the surgery and thinking how sick it looked. I remember looking at her flat chest with a scar after her mastectomy and thinking how healthy it looked. She has taken cancer in stride and never once let it overcome her. I wish I were as strong as she was.

Dialogue between Sheryl and Yael, September 2011

Yael: You want to say that shopping for bras after a mastectomy has not been difficult?

Sheryl: No, it has never been easier. Now I can finally find a bra that fits both of my boobs.

Yael: You never have sadness when you go shopping for a bra?

Sheryl: The loss associated with losing my right breast, which was substantially smaller and so made my bust asymmetrical, was not as traumatic as other experiences in my lifetime. When I was thirty years old, I was designing macramé jewelry and my livelihood, sense of self, and identity was focused on being able to create with my hands. I underwent two carpal tunnel surgeries that year and lost the full use of my hands for over six months. It was as if I lost the essence of my being.

It's hard to know how I would have felt if I had gone through a mastectomy at the age of forty-three with Breast Cancer 1, BC-1 as I call it. However, I know that at the time the only thing I was dealing with was losing a part of my breast, but not all of it. The reality was that after I had my lumpectomy and radiation, my right breast was no longer part of my sexuality. I lost sensation, and it was often painful to be touched, and the breast that was still there was a reminder of the illness. Also, I do not see myself without a breast on a daily basis. My bathroom mirror is too high for me to see my full chest. I only see my face, and because of living circumstances I very rarely look at myself in a full-size mirror.

Yael: It's not because of living circumstances. It's because you don't want to.

Sheryl: No, it's our living circumstances. Because we live in a small living area, I chose to have the mirror in the place where I look at myself when I am dressed just before I leave the house.

Yael: I am going to ask you again: Seriously, how many towels do you have? A dozen. How many blankets? One on every bed plus three or four extras. So you have extra for everything, so why don't you have a full-size mirror in the bedroom?

Sheryl: I'll tell you why.

Yael: There is no doubt in my mind you have an excuse.

Sheryl: It's because of the shape of the room. But, when I am visiting other people, I do look.

Yael: That doesn't count because when you are visiting others or are in hotels, your mood is totally different. It is not the daily mood, but a vacation, a once-in-a-lifetime opportunity.

Sheryl: Ok. If not having a boob really affected me, wouldn't you assume that I would always wear my prosthesis and bra and never be seen in private or public with only one boob? In all honesty, I hate bras and as soon as I get into the house I take my bra and boob off. It used to be only with my immediate family including Asaf, and now it has extended further. I will usually wear dark-colored clothes that do not accentuate one boob only, but I feel very comfortable at this point with anybody, although I do not go to work in a boob-less state.

The first time the bandages came off, I was alone in the house and I went into the bathroom and I set the mirror so I could see it. When I took the bandages off, I let out a one-second cry followed by, "Wow! She did an excellent job on the surgery." At this stage of my life, the loss of my breast is the gain of my life. Breast Cancer 2, BC-2, was diagnosed at early stages and did not require any follow-up treatments such as chemo and radiation. Thus, the removal of the breast was so much easier compared to BC-1. For me, it was moving on with my life knowing that the breast is gone and hopefully I will never have to deal with breast cancer on that side again. What did become important for me after BC-2 was finding ways to regain and maintain my physical strength in various ways and not only through swimming. As a result, I started rowing with We Can Row and dragon boating with the Wellness Warriors, both cancer survivor teams that have given me a whole new direction and allowed me to find new ways to express myself. Maybe I will get a full-length mirror and see how I feel.

Schlopping Tips

- Empower yourself with knowledge in order to make the best-informed decision that is appropriate for you.
- When making your decision, incorporate the different types of knowledge including: authoritative (professional); embodied (experience); technical (procedural); and traditional (folklore).
- Bad things happen, and you just need to move on.
- We don't always choose what happens to us, yet we choose how we cope with it.
- Love your boobs as they are at the moment, and love them even more when they change.

6. The Universal Fashion Show

"What do you think about this one?"

THE UNIVERSAL RITUAL AFTER BUYING CLOTHES is that one comes home and "does a fashion show." The fashion show is a way to brag about your new findings; a way to continue the schlopping euphoria; a way to get compliments when you think compliments should be given; a way to justify yourself for buying these new items; and, if applicable, a way to make up your mind whether to keep your purchases or return them.

Schlopping does not end at the stores. It continues on the way home when schlopping buddies talk about their purchases in the bags and what they like about them. They talk about the items that should have been in their bags but were left behind, probably because they deliberated too much and could not make up their minds. It is a way to let the euphoric feeling linger and to bring it into their homes. The actual fashion show, the ritual of what you do and with whom you do it, is one that should be cherished and nourished.

There are different questions concerning the strategy of one's fashion show. Where do you do the fashion show? Do you do it in front of your mirror alone? Do you do it in front of all the people in the house? Do you Skype others or use some other form of social media? Do you hide the things you bought? Do you try on your new items with old items in your closet? Do you try on the thing you like best the first? Do you regret your purchases? Are you angry at the salesperson?

Often, there are spectators, whether designated or just because they are in the house, who add a very important component. We have the need to ask others for their opinion and their approval. As a Tanzanian woman who grew up in the city once said to Sheryl, "After shopping I come home, and ask everyone in the house and it doesn't matter who, the housekeeper, the gardener or the cook, to sit and look at the clothes I bought."

Fashion shows with partners are not always easy. We come home with dozens of bags and they may react negatively to our purchases and insinuate that we should not have bought all those items or spent so much money. They may say: "Did you leave anything in the store?" "How much did you spend?" "Where are you going to put all these things?" "Don't you already have the same thing?" "Do you really need an extra pair of black pants?" "Don't you already have a lot of shoes? You can only wear one pair at a time." The response may be: "But I saved 35 percent." "I didn't buy half the things I wanted to buy." "You should see how much our neighbor just spent on clothes." "They were all on sale: buy two get two free." "I have to have something to wear to see your parents next week." "I just gained twenty pounds and nothing fits." Our partners' remarks are often about money and make us feel as if we did something wrong. These remarks will bring us down after the high note of our schlopping trip. Some people hide their purchases as a way to protect themselves and avoid these comments.

The fashion show may leave you with ambivalent feelings because sometimes you buy an item that you really like and think looks good on you, yet receive negative reactions from the spectators, while sometimes the items you like the least are complimented the most.

Often, we want to see ourselves in our own mirrors. After all, many times our reflection in the mirror in the store differs from the one in our own home. Some say that the mirrors in the fitting rooms have optical effects that, together with the lighting, make the person in the reflection look slimmer and taller. We want to know whether our potential new purchases look as good as we thought they did when we were in front of the dressing room mirror.

The fashion show is also the last step in schlopping: the next time you put the new garment on your body it will be "getting dressed" with an item in your wardrobe rather than schlopping.

Sheryl: I start by taking out all the new items from the bags and laying them on my bed. Then I try on one new item at a time and will go into my closet to retrieve an old item in order to see if I can create a new outfit. Even when I am in the dressing room in the store, I start thinking of the items already in my wardrobe that will match the new purchase. Once I came home and put on a new blouse with an old pair of pants that I had been wearing for the past year and asked Sam what he thought. His comment was, "I like the blouse, but the pants don't look good on you. Take them back." He didn't even notice that I had worn the pants for the last year.

In 1926, after my maternal grandparents, Gommie and Granddaddy, married, they opened up a dry goods clothing store in the small town of Columbus, Texas, named Klein's. They carried almost everything to clothe their children and later their grandchildren. When we were growing up, schlopping at the store was one of the most exciting things we did on Sunday mornings and holidays when the family would gather together. We, the women in the family, would take the keys to the store and go and spend several hours rummaging through the racks and trying on anything and everything we thought we might like. These schlopping expeditions often included my mom, her sister Maxine, her sister-in-law Lolly, my cousin Lisa, and I. We would begin with dresses, shirts, and pants and then move on to the accessories to find the jewelry and purses to match. There were years during which the only things we ever bought in retail clothing stores were bras and shoes! We would be in and out of the dressing rooms, pulling clothes off the racks and trying on everything that was in our size, just to see how it looked. Our grandparents set two stipulations to these schlopping trips: one, we always had to hang the clothes back on the hangers; and two, we had to wear what we took. To this day, whenever I shop in a clothing store, I obsessively hang everything back on hangers, just the way I found it; some habits are never broken. As to wearing everything that I buy, that is not always the case.

By the time we got home with our chosen items, Gommie had already prepared lunch for everyone and Granddaddy and the other men had completed their eighteen holes of golf. Upon our return, the fashion show was now for the rest of the family, and we would parade in front of everyone to see their reactions. All the women would go into Gommie and Granddaddy's bedroom, and we would put all the items on the bed and start to try on, one by one, all the things that we took from the store. We would each put on a new outfit and go out to the family den for the scrutiny of the whole family. The comment I always received was, "It looks so cute on you!" Even as I enter into my seventh decade, people still tell me I look cute. I call myself vertically challenged, given my four-feet-nine height. I assume that people would not be saying, "Cute!" to a five-feet-nine-tall woman.

In 1974, two years after we were married, my husband, Sam and I took a trip from our home in Israel to America to visit family in New York and Texas. Since we were married in Israel and the extended family was not at our wedding, my grandparents planned a large garden party in our honor and I needed something new to wear. As usual, Sam went golfing with the men and the ladies went to my grandparents' store to schlop. We all came home with our bundles of clothes and started our typical fashion show. There was one outfit, a one-piece blouse-and-shorts romper set, that everyone said looked so cute on me. But Sam hated it and said, "It makes you look like a *little girl*."

There was quite a bit of tension, conflict, and "loud discussions" with my grandmother, mother, and aunts, who all thought I should wear it to the party. Sam, being the opinionated person he is, was adamantly against it, especially because everyone thought I looked so cute. He saw me as a mature woman, even though I was only twenty-three. Gommie, the Sargent Major of the family, was not used to anyone disagreeing with her, especially about clothes. Here I was caught in the middle: the women matriarchs in my family thought one thing and my husband another. So whom should I listen to? What should I do? Sam won the battle of the fashion show, and I did not wear the outfit to the party. However, I kept it so as not to insult Gommie, and I actually liked the outfit. Whenever I would wear it, Sam would express his negative opinion and I would just think back to the party and the humorous tension that often exists around the choice of clothes.

In 1985, exactly a year after my father passed away, I went to Tel Aviv, the big city, to have a day to myself. It had been a very difficult year in many ways, especially mourning the loss of my father, who had passed away suddenly at the age of six-ty-four. As usual, I gravitated to the open-air market that sold clothes and found several hand-stitched embroidered shirts and matching skirts of Indian tie-dye cotton. I then went to the garment district on Allenby Street, where the small bou-tique stores are lined up and down the street. After trying on several things, I found the most beautiful turquoise harem pants and an oversized blouse with large patterned flowers and colors that coordinated with the pants. The store owner recommended a wide black soft leather belt that closed at the hip, allowing the blouse to gently drape over the pants.

I had been told all my life not to wear contrasting color belts at the waist, because they "cut you in two and make you look shorter." As I stood in front of the mirror and gazed at myself, I saw an image of a new person, so I kept on those clothes and walked out of the store feeling like a million dol-lars. When I got home and started my fashion show, Sam's comment was, "How much did you spend on those clothes? You know we don't have any money." To say the least, I was very upset. Part of his response was related to the monetary factor, because we were on a very tight budget at that time. Yet the clothes I had bought were reasonably priced. Here I was, choosing to do something for myself to feel better after a year of mourning for my father, and yet I was made to feel guilty that I had spent money.

Why do some partners do that and say those things? Is it their way to control us, even when we are also working and contributing to the fiscal family unit? Here I had purchased myself a few new clothes and was feeling like a million dollars, yet the reaction was as though I had spent a million dollars. After that incident, for many years to follow, not only did I feel guilty for spending money on myself, but also I learned to hide the clothes and other things I bought and would not always want to have the fashion show with Sam, fearing his reactions.

In 2010, two years after my mastectomy, I had one of my best fashion shows in my life. Before I lost my boob, I always used to buy blouses in styles that hid my cleavage and bust. After Breast Cancer 2, I finally got up the courage to buy new-style blouses that were tight, v-necked with a rather low cut, and made of material that clings to the body. I started the fashion show by choosing the safest pick, a green and blue blouse that I bought in the exact same style that I had previously bought in other colors. Sam loved that blouse, and I continued the fashion show. Then I put on the same-style shirt in black and gray. I really liked the slick lines, yet Sam did not like it all. My first reaction was to put it back in the bag for return. However, instead, I went to my closet and put on a mid-knee skirt and mid-calf boots, both bought the previous winter yet never worn and still having the tags on, to complete the look. When I came out to the living room, Sam loved the look and told me, "You look amazing."

As I gazed into the mirror, I saw in front of me a rather beautiful and sexy woman and decided that I actually liked that blouse and the only thing missing was that I would now have to make a color coordinated macramé necklace to hang in the crevice of the low v-neckline. Today, now that I have two boobs that are the same size, I have gained a sense of boob-self that gives me the freedom to wear low-cut and tight-fitting clothes as never before.

Yael: Putting on the first garment is always like trying on the first wedding dress. There is the "wow factor"—that you look beautiful because you look different. After the first two garments, come all of the other garments that often are much more scrutinized and compared to the ones before them. The fashion show for me is a way to reaffirm my decision, which has often been made in the dressing room at the store, in front of the mirror.

On a cold bright day in February 2011, my mom and I went schlopping unintentionally. We were downtown at a meeting, and we just happened to go into the Macy's "just to look," and we lucked out. For us, "lucking out" means that the items we wanted to buy were on sale. A rack of cocktail and formal dresses was filled with dresses of all sizes, shapes, and colors and it was beckoning for us to go through and pick out items. We went into the dressing room with the maximum allowable items and clothes started to fly in all directions.

I was luckily and happily pregnant for the second time, and my brother-in-law was getting married in April and I needed a dress. I was about four months pregnant, and I wanted to buy a tight-fitting dress that would show both the beautiful baby bump as well as my beautiful body. I was looking forward to the fluctuation of my body shape and it was one of the happiest times I have had in my life in a dressing room.

I was anticipating that finding a dress would take a long time, but I was pleasantly surprised that even the first dress I put on fit me really well and showed off the budding of the belly. I put a T-shirt on my belly to see if the dress could hold the stretching of my body and the racks of "yes," "maybe," and "no" started to overflow. We bought a dozen dresses, in various sizes, including dresses that were full price with the intent to return the unwanted. As soon as we got home, I gathered everyone in the house and made them look at every garment I put on.

To make sure the spectators complimented the items that I wanted, I showed those items at the beginning of the fashion show, when the wow factor was still intact. The first item I put on was a garment I knew I wanted to keep, but not necessarily wear for the wedding. I received rave reviews from the audience and felt on top of the world. Although I did not wear it for the wedding, I wore it when I was nine months pregnant, when I hosted a Fourth of July party for Asaf's Masonic lodge as well as for my daughter's baby-naming ceremony three weeks postpartum. The second item in the fashion show was the first dress I put on in the dressing room; I really liked it for the wedding. Its wow factor outshone the first item in the fashion show, and all agreed that that was the dress for the wedding. Only at the end did I put on the dresses that were not on sale. By the time we reached the end of the fashion show, the wow factor had subsided, and the dresses not on sale were not more beautiful than the dresses on sale. I kept three items from that trip, all of which had been on sale, and returned all the rest to the store.

With new technology, the fashion show has now evolved. One day my mom went shopping during a snow storm, and although we were only fifteen minutes away, we decided to use Skype for the fashion show. We are living now in Boston and my in-laws are still in Israel, so often I Skype with my mother-in-law while both of us do our fashion shows. Two weddings and another baby-naming ceremony had taken place in the family and we had been able to share the experience of choosing outfits for each occasion with each other even though we were six thousand miles apart. When she came to visit us in America and bought presents to take back to the family in Israel, I encouraged her to go on Skype with her daughter before returning to make sure her daughter liked the items. It was strange for her to buy with the intention of taking back the unwanted. She is used to shopping in a country that doesn't have a return policy. She did not shop to return; she always shopped to buy. Her policy is to buy the items, take off the tags, hang them in her closet, and use them the next day or event. She never has bags with merchandise waiting to be returned to the stores, as my mom and I have.

One of the most memorable fashion shows took place in the winter of 2009, about six months after I had my son. I went schlopping with my mom and we bought dozens of clothes: we bought jeans, sweaters, blouses, shoes, and boots. I had already lost some of my baby weight. After months of studying and taking care of my baby and not really taking time to treat myself, this was the first time I had gone shopping for a very long time. When we got into the car after piling all the bags in the trunk and thought about the fashion show I would do, I said to Mom, "Now I feel beautiful again." Her reaction was filled with happiness and sadness. She was happy because I felt beautiful, but she was sad because she understood that if I said "again" it meant that for a while I hadn't felt beautiful. That evening, she came home with me and I did a fashion show trying on all the new items I had bought in front of Asaf, my baby, and Mom. It lasted over an hour and I felt like a million bucks.

In 2013, our home was blessed with two holidays occurring at the same time, Thanksgiving and Chanukah, or as it came to be called, Thanksgivukkah. Our home was warm with people, food, and light and we were four generations spending time together. We ate turkey, cranberry sauce, and sweet potatoes for an early dinner and *latkes* and Chanukah doughnuts for dessert. The stove was lit the whole day and the candles in the menorah were lit at night.

Before the football game started, the kids watched with their great-grandmother the original Disney *Snow White* movie from 1938. Both generations knew the songs and hummed the whole time in harmony. It is amazing how memories are created and stored in our brains for eternity.

After the movie, all four generations of women went to the kitchen to finish the final touches. While my mom was skimming the fat off the soup with the huge stainless steel spoon she had taken from her grandmother's house, she started reminiscing about the family Thanksgiving tradition of schlopping in the family store and doing fashion shows. I realized that they, as a family, had adopted shopping as a tradition on Thanksgiving more than fifty years ago. We started talking whether stores should be open on Thanksgiving Day, because that year many stores had decided for the first time to open on the holiday or to open earlier than in previous years. As family members of store owners and salespeople, we thought about how awful it was for people who had to leave their families and go to work. Still, even given that reservation, we understood the desire of many families who wish to shop together on that day. All we could hope was that those who wanted to be home were home with their families and friends and those who wanted to shop or work were at the stores.

At this point, my daughter was dressing her great-grandmother with all the bracelets and necklaces she could find in the house. They both were thrilled to connect to each other on that level and share the experience in that moment. It was gratifying to see both women, young and old, sharing the love of dressing up. On this Thanksgivukkah, I wanted to know Savta's strategy for the fashion show.

It is hard for Savta to speak long sentences because Parkinson's disease has diminished her ability to control her jaw muscles. So I spoke to her like I used to speak to my kids when they were one year old and knew only a few words. I asked her, "Savta, what was your strategy in the fashion show? Did you use to put on the favorite one first or the one that…" But I couldn't finish my sentence because as soon as I said "favorite one first," her eyes lit up and her lips grinned and I knew that that was the answer. I said with a smile and a nod of my head, "So, the one you loved most? That's what you put on first?" and she softly, slowly, firmly, and happily said, "Yes." She made the same sound as my children make when they know the word or answer. And so another piece of the puzzle for me was filled, as I learned the fashion-show strategy of the best dresser I know.

Schlopping Tips

- Have fun with the fashion show, and don't over-analyze it.
- Keep the items you feel good in, even if others don't like them.
- As a spectator, be honest but don't rain on anyone's parade.
- As a partner, try not to make sarcastic remarks about the shopping. It will harm your relationship.
- Often, the first or second item you put on will receive the most positive reviews.
- Try to observe and understand nonverbal communication.

7. The Price Of Schlopping

**"Schlopping with my grandchildren is a way
to create memories."**

Schlopping can be a very pricy activity on all levels, monetarily as well as emotionally. There are times that shopping can cause tension and conflict between schlopping buddies who do not agree on what to purchase and what looks nice. There are families in which money is not an issue and one can spend endlessly without restrictions and other homes where there may be a lack of financial backing and everyone is on a tight budget. There are kids who want expensive things and parents who cannot afford it. There are parents who want to buy expensive things, but kids do not want to feel the responsibility that goes along with those purchases. Money and purchases affect relationships and we must learn how to deal with them so that they do not bankrupt us or others emotionally or financially.

Sheryl: Barbara has been my closest schlopping buddy for years. We shopped together all the time, for special events in our lives, when I was undergoing chemotherapy, and after every visit to the dentist. Somehow, after spending hours under sedation and undergoing procedures such as root canals, bone grafting, and gum surgeries, we just needed to get together and shop!

During one of our schlopping trips together, Barbara went into the dressing room and started to try on several outfits. She finally found a dress that she absolutely loved. But to me, it looked more like a sailor outfit than a dress suitable for a mother of four teenage children. It was a shirtwaist dress with a large collar in apricot color. I tried to be tactful and to give her my honest opinion and recommended that she try on another dress. For some reason she was very persistent and wanted that particular dress so much that she had the *chutzpah*, audacity, to actually kick me out of the dressing room. Barbara was always caring and polite to everyone, so her behavior caught me off guard. She said to me, "Just leave the store, and let's meet in half an hour for lunch." To say the least, I was quite offended. Because we never had arguments or disagreements, being told that she did not want my opinion about a dress felt like a slap in the face. We always shopped together and often depended on one another to get the required compliments and to make our final decisions. In the end, she bought that hideous dress. Yet a few days later, she took it back and exchanged it for two other items, a sweater and a blouse that she wore for years. In fact, just recently we spoke about that incident, which happened more than twenty years ago, and we just laughed how we both remember that schlopping trip as if it were yesterday.

I had a similar experience with Sam when he once came on a schlopping trip with me. It was soon after my chemotherapy, and my body still had a rather round shape. So I was very limited in the clothes that I could wear, choosing to wear baggy, frumpy clothes that covered my midriff bulges. I started to try on various items, and each time I came out of the dressing room to show him, his comment was something like, "It's too big, it makes you look shorter and wider," or, "I don't like the style." The salespeople kept saying they looked great—of course, what else could they say, they were trying to make a sale—and Sam kept telling me how terrible everything looked. I was both exhausted by Sam's comments and rather embarrassed about his behavior, so I chose to leave the store; it was evident that it would be impossible to purchase any items with him by my side. A few days later, I returned alone to the same store, and the salesperson said, "Great! You came alone without your husband." To this day, Sam still claims that they tried to sell me clothing that was not suitable for my body and I have just accepted that it is often best not to take him shopping with me and just leave him at home.

When Yael was in her twenties, we went shopping on her birthday. I bought her dozens of items worth hundreds of dollars. I wanted to splurge and buy her special things on this particular birthday as a way to pamper her because we had all gone through financial difficulties that year. After the schlopping trip, I went home on a train and she called me on my cell phone upset and crying about her guilty feelings concerning me spending so much money on her. All I wanted to do was to make her feel good on her birthday. Yet, unbeknown to me, it instead made her feel worse.

When I was growing up, although we never had a lot of money, we always had *more* clothes than others did, probably because Gommie and Granddaddy had their clothing store. You could say we lived comfortably and were able to buy within reason and had most things we wanted. To place us on a scale, we were middle class and lived in an ok neighborhood, and while there were those who lived much better with more money and more cars, there were others who were less fortunate than we were.

My father was the breadwinner and the sole financial supporter of our family while Mom was a stay-at-home mom, as was typical in the 1950s and 1960s in the community where I grew up in Houston, Texas. The only moms I knew who worked outside the home were teachers, nurses, in a family business, or those who had to work for financial reasons. In other words, men were expected to provide for their families in order that their wives could stay at home to run the household and take care of the kids. During my childhood, I would frequently shop with my mom and we usually were able to purchase the items that we liked.

In my early teens, due to an unexpected family illness, we went through very difficult financial times and had to make substantial changes for several years. My parents tried to hide it from us. But as teenagers, we were old enough to decipher the quiet talk about not being able to buy certain things, and we knew that we would have to go to work to make pocket money in order to buy nonessential items. One day, I accidentally saw my parents' checkbook. There were red numbers and a minus dollar value. I felt a sense of panic. I remember that once Mom and I went to buy clothes at Battelstein's, the store where Dad worked, and the credit card was rejected. It was soon after that incident that I felt I had to take care of myself. Yet I most likely did not fully understand the financial situation. The hush-hush in the house about the change in our economic status created an undertone that had a great effect on my life and the way I started to look at shopping.

For as long as I can remember, I used to find ways to make money, whether through babysitting, setting up lemonade stands, selling gift cards around the neighborhood, or wrapping gifts and making bows during the holiday season at my grandparents' store. At the age of fifteen, I was able to get my first real paying job as a gift-wrapper at Battelstein's department store. At the time, my father was the manager of the men's department, so, due to nepotism, I was able to start working before I was sixteen, the typical age to get a part-time job. I was already an experienced gift-wrapper and was excellent at the job. After the holiday season, I was promoted to work as a cashier and continued to work part-time throughout my high school years.

As a result of the family hardships, I stopped asking my parents for money and for several years I limited shopping for clothes to items needed only for special occasions, rather than bought for pleasure, as Mom and I had done for years. I felt guilty if I had to ask for money, and this guilt stayed with me for many years to come. As I mentioned before, due to my height, I was very short waisted and the styles of that time were a challenge to wear because they mostly accentuated a small waistline. As a result, from the age of thirteen, when I got my first sewing machine, I started to sew most of my own clothes. I could make clothes that actually fit my body type, and it was also a way to overcome financial hardship, as it was cheaper to make clothes than to purchase them.

This also had a great effect on my attitudes and habits of shopping. In addition to buying only essential items, I kept clothes and other things forever. This has certainly been a problem of mine, and to this day I cannot get rid of things or part with clothes. While Yael and I were discussing this issue, we both looked at one another and just laughed, because this is a problem we both have. For some reason, even decades later, I find it very hard, almost impossible, to throw out old clothes. I just keep things hanging in my closet for years, even clothes that are too big or too small, because I never know if I might gain or lose weight. Some of my clothes are out of style, yet we all know that if you keep them long enough, they come back into fashion, as have Indian tie-dye skirts and hand-embroidered shirts.

Part of it is also due to fear that one day I may not be able to afford to buy new things, and another factor is that somehow it has been engrained in me not to waste, not to throw away, and to wear clothes for years. So many times I have looked at the racks of clothes in my closet and said to myself, "I don't have anything to wear." I once tried a new strategy and decided that for every new garment, I would remove three articles of clothing. I thought that would reduce the clutter. Although that did work for a while, I soon returned to my old pattern of buying without discarding.

A lot of these patterns developed as I was growing up under the influence of the American consumer culture that the customer is always right, everything is returnable, and there is a money-back guarantee. This shopping culture means that you can buy anything you want, take it home, and then return it, often no questions asked. Shopping in America is not a decisive activity: you have a right to change your mind, and that is how I learned to shop from a very young age from my mom. Whether it was in my grandparents' store in Columbus or in a major department store, we could buy clothes on credit, bring things home to try on, and return what we didn't like. In fact, until today, I often avoid shopping at "Final Sales, No Returns" sales because the idea that I cannot reverse a decision and might be left with a piece of clothing that looked good in the store in the dressing room, yet different in front of the mirror at home, inflicts a burden on me. I have a hard time shopping even on vacations, as I know once I buy an item I cannot return it. It is only on the last day, when I understand I have to make a final decision, that I make my last schlopping trip in that city, going from store to store again and purchasing the items I saw throughout the trip.

When I moved to Israel in 1969, at the age of eighteen to study abroad, I went through a shopping culture shock because I did not know how to shop in an environment where you could not go into a store to just try on clothes or to buy and return. In fact, according to the Code of Jewish Law, *Shulchan Aruch*, there is a prohibition against inquiring about the price of an item if you are not interested in making a purchase. In those days, there were not any shopping malls in Israel. The only stores were small Mom-and-Pop stores, and it was offensive and unethical to go in just to look or to try on clothes without the intent to buy. In addition, there were no return policies at all, not in any type of store and certainly not in the open-air bazaar markets. I rarely bought clothes, and on the rare occasions when I did need to purchase things, I often spent hours deliberating because I knew that I had only one chance to decide; once I paid the money, there could be no regrets.

In addition, I was again on a very limited budget for many years and learned to buy only essentials and developed the habit of keeping things forever, recycling, and never throwing anything away. I took old sheets and converted them to duvet covers, or cut them up for pillowcases. I designed skirts from old blue jeans, darned socks, turned around frayed collars on shirts to get extra years of wear, repaired heels or broken straps on shoes, and kept clothes forever.

Even as I married and had children, these attitudes and behavioral patterns continued for years. When our children were young, we often skimped and bought cheap clothes and second-hand furniture in the flea markets so we could spend the little money we had on the children's education and enrichment activities and occasional trips to America to visit family. These trips were a way for the grandparents and grandchildren to spend time together, which always included schlopping trips for clothes and toys and visits to museums, parks, and zoos and even once to Disney World. One of my strategies when I traveled to America was to pack a minimum amount of clothes in an oversize suitcase: I knew that any item I didn't bring would legitimize buying a new item. I needed the additional luggage on the return trip to take back all the purchases from our schlopping expeditions.

My parents were very secretive about their financial situation, so, as a result, I tried to do it differently when I became a parent. I felt that letting our children know that we did not have a lot of money would help them understand the value of money and would protect them from being caught off guard, as I was when I saw the red in the checkbook so many years ago. Although we always told our kids that we had enough to provide for them, we told them that prioritizing is the key and that we do not have a lot of money for extra things, such as expensive furniture, fine jewelry, expensive clothes, or other nonessential things.

By 1980, the macramé jewelry that I designed and sold at arts and crafts fairs had taken its toll on my hands and I was diagnosed with severe carpel tunnel syndrome. I underwent surgery on both hands. I was unable to work for over a year, and since my livelihood was dependent on creating with my hands, this caused financial hardship for our family. Several months after the second surgery, we moved to Davis, California, so Sam could accept a two-year postdoctorate position.

Soon after our arrival, we took our children, who were three and five at the time, to Toys"R"Us and told them that we did not have enough money to buy anything; we were only going to look. They had never seen such a large toy store, and these little children were in awe of the rows and rows of toys. They behaved in an amazing manner for young children and understood that we were not going there to buy. They therefore didn't ask to purchase even one item. I felt that our teaching had succeeded.

Today, with my own grandchildren, who are now three and five, there are times that I try to take them into Toys"R"Us and let them sit in the kid-size cars, look at the toys, and enjoy the experience without purchasing anything—although I can never resist and buy them at least one small item. I love to take them schlopping and watch their decision-making process and wait patiently for them to choose the special thing they want to buy. It is as if I have to shop with them everywhere we go together, even at museums, the supermarket, or a CVS. It is funny to me that I am doing it differently as a grandparent than as a parent; when my kids were growing up, we did not purchase things everywhere we went. I also take pleasure in having enough financial stability that I can spend money on items for them when I go shopping by myself. Yael often gets mad at me when I buy them so many toys and books and requests that I stop and control myself. She also tells me that I am creating the habit of always purchasing things for them wherever they go, which may not always be the best lesson. Yet, often I cannot resist the urge to buy them gifts in order to see the joy on their face when I give them their presents or shop with them. I love it when they say, "This is the best present ever!" and they give me a huge hug and kiss; it is worth every penny.

Yael: When we were growing up, my parents were always on a tight budget. I still remember them sitting Yotam and me down when he was ten and I was eight, telling us that they did not have a lot of money and we needed to stop buying popsicles at the local store. It was on that day that I began to feel responsible for my parents' financial well-being, and I think it affected my psyche for life.

Although they did not have a lot of money, they always wanted us to have things that we needed and sent us to extracurricular activities such as music and dance. They would say that spending money is about prioritizing and they always had enough for our education and future. Even though we had little money, our household had more things than all of my other friends' households; we always had more clothes, accessories, shoes, pictures on the walls, books, kitchen items, and a pantry full of extra items, "just in case."

But although we had more "stuff," in some ways we had less. We never went on vacations, except to visit family, or had cable TV, or the latest technology such as a VCR at that time. My parents viewed those things as less important than other things. When they took us to special events to broaden our horizons and enrich our lives, the goal was to spend as little as possible. We always ate before we left home, often took food with us in order to "not waste money on food," and if a drink was purchased, Yotam and I shared. We never bought memorabilia from the event because my parents used to say, "Everything is too expensive, and the experience alone is enough." Often, I was embarrassed. But in the big picture, I knew that my parents had enough money to support us comfortably and felt proud that they were successful.

When my kids were four and two, my husband and I took them to the *Cavalia* horse show. We were on a very tight budget and opted for cheap tickets. As we walked up the stairs to our seats, I saw an usher talking to a family and handing them tickets. This jogged a memory of my own from when I was a teenager and my mom and I went to a U2 concert on October 14, 1992, in the old Astrodome in Houston, Texas.

We of course bought the cheapest tickets. It was Row 58, and, unbeknown to us at the time of purchase, had an obstructed view from behind a projector. Looking down at the stage was like seeing little tiny ants walking around; we were closer to the roof than the stage.

Before the show started, my mom saw an usher exchanging tickets with other people and went to him and asked, "What are you doing?" He said, "They are filming this concert and want young women to be in the first row." She said, "My daughter and I have an obstructed view, so could we please exchange tickets? We're young women." After gazing at us, he said, "Follow me." I still remember walking all the way down the numerous ramps in the stadium from one level to the next until we reached the main floor by the stage. At this point, he gave us two tickets and said, "Keep going forward." We had no idea that the tickets he had given us were front row, center stage. As we reached our seats, we were amazed and thrilled and could not believe this had happened to us. The guy who sat next to me asked, "When did you buy your ticket? I sat in line all night five months ago to buy them." With a huge grin and a little sense of embarrassment, I said, "Oh, just yesterday, but we got tickets for the fifty-eighth row and got upgraded." My mom still talks with pride of how the *schvitz*, or sweat, of Bono touched her forehead and I think she did not wash it for days. As usual, I did not purchase anything at the show, but I still have the ticket stub, the fake one-dollar bills that were thrown to the audience during the performance of the song

"One," and the clip-on "Vote" pin that was thrown during the opening act by Public Enemy.

And so, as the parent this time around at the *Cavalia* horse show, after seeing an usher giving out tickets to others, I approached and asked her, "Are you upgrading by any chance? Do you have better seats for me and my kids?" She replied with a smile, "Sure, how many do you need?" We were upgraded to the best seats in the venue, eighth-row, center stage. We were thrilled.

At the intermission, we each took a child to the bathroom and on the way could not avoid looking at the over-priced merchandise. The same record played in my head, and this time as a parent as we passed the merchandise, I told my child, "We cannot buy anything, but only look." I let my daughter look at all the items. Like a pro, she said, "Let me see everything they have. I want to choose." She opted for a soft, medium-white horse that cost fifty-five dollars and was clutching the doll with a huge smile on her face. I informed her, again, with a heavy heart, that it was too expensive to buy.

A woman heard me, approached me, and said, "If I give you $30, will you have the other $25 for the doll?" and handed me the money. I froze. How could I take money from a stranger to buy my child a toy? I never even had dates pay for me. And even if I did take the money and spent "only" $25, which I thought was a lot of money for a stuffed animal, it meant I would also have to spend the same amount of money for my son to buy a toy and we would have "wasted" over $250 including the tickets to see horses dance ballet.

As I politely rejected her money, she told me that she had never been lucky enough to have beautiful children like mine, she had just turned sixty years old, and this would be one of her birthday presents to herself. I continued rejecting the money, but she just stuck the money in my pocket, said, "Pay it forward," and left. Her friend stayed behind and said, "Let her do this; she does this all the time and it makes her happy." I handed the money back to her friend and said, "I cannot accept this," but she refused to take it and then walked away.

I had never taken money from a stranger before. Just the opposite: I was raised to give to others who were less fortunate, and all my life I was at the other end of giving to strangers. I did what I often do when making decisions and weighed the options against each other. If I declined the money, my pride and wallet would stay intact, my child would not have a toy, and the woman could not do what she loves to do. If I took the money, my pride and wallet would be hurt, my child would have a toy, and the woman would do what she loves to do. It was as if by accepting the money, I was the only one who would be hurt and the rest would only benefit from this act. I went against all my instincts and pride and took the money. While I was giving the cashier those bills, my hands shook and my heart was filled with happiness, anxiety, and anticipation of what this purchase meant and the happiness that it would bring to us.

Obviously, we had to purchase a toy for my son, who chose a horse on a stick, which was forty-five dollars. They have played with these horses for endless hours and often go to sleep with them at night. My son named his horse Sleepy because his horse fell asleep at the show, and my daughter named her horse Artax the Horsey after the horse in *The Never Ending Story*, the movie they had just seen. They are beautiful toys, as well they should for their price, but at this point they are priceless. The joy they bring to my kids when they play with them, and the memories of the show when we reminisce, will stay with them and us forever. It is as if this woman not only helped buy toys and create memories for my kids, but also helped break the record of buying special things at events. I now understand that sometimes "wasting" the extra money in special places is worth every penny.

Six months later, my son and I went to the park and on the way back he wanted a treat. I put my hand in my pocket and found only a quarter. I told him, "We only have twenty-five cents so you need to choose an item for that price." When we shop with our kids for toys, clothes, or presents for others, we often give them a budget and they need to find something accordingly. As they go through the rows, they ask, "Does this cost X?" and if it is too expensive, yet they really like the toy, they will say, "Maybe I will buy this for my birthday." So my son understood the concept of a budget, and we walked into the store and asked the cashier what he had for twenty-five cents. He said he had nothing for that price. I was shocked, as usually they have at least a piece of candy for a quarter. My son was sad and was holding a tiny piece of chocolate. A young male college student who was in the store paid for the treat without my knowledge and then told us, "I just paid for

it. Take it and enjoy it." The student had done what I have
done so many times in my life.

I told my son to give the student the quarter he had, but
the stranger declined and left. It did not feel right to keep the
money, so I told my son, "Let's take this twenty-five cents and
'pay it forward.' 'Pay it forward' is when somebody does something nice for you and you do something nice for somebody
else. Let's find a homeless person and give him the money."
He loved the idea, and so we were on a mission to find a
homeless person in need. We talked about homeless people,
where they lived, and why it is important to help. He asked
me about shelters and whether homeless people have food
and toys.

We walked around Kenmore Square in Boston for twenty-five minutes and could not find one homeless person,
which was very unusual. It is amazing how when you want
something, it is never in sight. We were so disappointed and
it started to rain and so we headed back home. As we crossed
the street, I glanced one last time at the corner and finally saw
the homeless person who was regularly there walking back
to his station. I told my son, "The homeless person is back,"
and we turned around to approach him. My son was thrilled
and as he gave his money to the person he was beaming with
happiness and pride and could not wait to go home and tell
his dad about it.

When Asaf heard the story, he was mortified that I let our
child take money or candy from a stranger. He was right: that
was a bad lesson and we reaffirmed to him that he can only

take food from strangers when mommy or daddy are with him. My husband said, "You should never do that," talking about taking money and candy from a stranger, but my son heard something else and yelled emphatically back to him, "I will *never* stop paying it forward." The feeling he got from giving something that he had to somebody in need was so powerful to him that he was even willing to disobey his parent to do what he thought was the right thing. The way he yelled that he would never stop paying it forward was filled with emotion and was amazing as a parent to hear. I asked him, "What was better, eating the candy or paying it forward?" After he thought for a minute, he said, "Both." What more could a parent ask from their child?

When we are on a tight budget, we can still receive priceless memories and experiences. Sometimes, to gain happiness for others we need to give up our own pride. I only hope that the woman who gave us money for the horses and the young college student who paid for the treat went home that day feeling satisfied that they had made a young child happy. They both changed our lives forever. The woman taught me that it is ok to receive from others and also that at special events, buying an expensive memorabilia item may bring priceless memories that could not be gained by buying the same item in a regular shop for a cheaper price. The young student gave me the opportunity to teach my son the concept of paying it forward. Although, we have taught him the concept of giving to those who are less fortunate and he has gathered toys in a box several times to give to hurricane survivors and children in shelters, this was the first time I had the opportunity to teach him to do something nice for others especially after someone has done something nice for you. Not only did he understand it, but he loved it and is willing to fight for it. Thus, when purchasing or receiving items, we need to think not only of their monetary price at that time but also of the value and lessons they will bring to us in life.

My dad is never selfish and rarely splurges on himself except for the Mont Blanc gold-tip fountain pens that he loves. As a professor and creator of ideas, writing is part of his self-image and he loves having his special pens. Spending his time and money on his family is and always has been his top priority. As he says, "What is life worth without doing all you can for your family?" My dad always shares everything he has, especially food, with everyone in the house: whenever he peels an orange or cuts an apple, the first thing he does is ask if anybody wants some. Often he is left with one slice of fruit for himself, but a heart full of love.

When my mom and I would come home from shopping with dozens of bags, the first thing Mom would say to him was, "Most of these are for your daughter," at which he would smile and say, "Great!" He even participates in the fashion show, and, although he gets bored at times, he always finds a way to stay focused and make us feel he is interested. He does not understand why people buy to return; he shops fast, in and out, and almost never returns. His fashion show is done in the store while shopping for the items. My brother, Yotam, on the other hand, loves shopping and loves buying presents especially for his niece and nephew. Even if he does not have a lot of money, he will often go to a second-hand store and buy the kids a toy or a garment "just because." I don't know who is happier when the kids open their presents, my brother or my children.

My dad loves taking his grandchildren schlopping, especially to the supermarket and to the local Barnes & Noble bookstore. His favorite thing to do while schlopping with his children and grandchildren is to show off his offspring. He loves talking to everyone about us and enjoys teaching us the little things in life. He always knows the salespeople by their first names and greets them with a smile. Everyone in the supermarket knows him and what he buys. I remember once my mom went to the supermarket and ordered sliced cheese and the salesperson said, "That is not what your husband buys." My mom changed her order and requested the "usual Sam."

He always does the household food shopping, thinks of all the people in the family, and buys their favorite bread, dessert, or drink. My mom always calls him dozens of times after he leaves the house to update the shopping list. He never says a word and gets her what she wants even if he needs to make three trips to the store. I think he likes being the person that brings my mom any and every food she desires so she can prepare a great family meal for all of us.

He taught me always to be kind to salespeople and know them by their names because that is the right thing to do. He always taught me to give to others and give spare change to homeless people who cross my path. He always says, "Life is what you make of it and you must look toward the future and not dwell on the past." And so, today I hope my children will learn from my dad what I learned from him while shopping with him: Life is fun and filled with endless people and opportunities waiting for you to enjoy them.

Dialogue between Yael and her dad, Sam, January, 2014

Yael: I feel like taking your grandchildren shopping is a way to connect and bond to them as well as show them off.

Sam: You forget one important thing: the sense of mortality I have as a grandparent. Grandparents don't know how much more time they have left with their grandchildren. It could be another minute or it could be another twenty years. Going shopping with them is not only a way for me to spend time with my grandchildren but also a way to give them something that they can hold on to and remember me by. I want them to have good memories of me and enjoy the things that I buy knowing that I might not be here later. When I take my grandchildren food shopping with me, it's an experience that connects me to them in their day-to-day life. I hope that when they go the supermarket when they are grown up they will remember the times they spent shopping with their Saba.

Yael: What is your favorite part of shopping with them?

Sam: When I have one kid with me, it's wonderful to see how that child is always so concerned about getting a present for the other one. Taking your kids shopping is also an occasion for me to do something wonderful for you, my daughter, by being with your kids as well as a way for me to see the great job you are doing. It is interesting how, as a grandparent, I have concerns and responsibilities, but very little power. After all, the grandkids are your kids, not mine.

Yael: Where do you like shopping with them?

Sam: Everywhere. Part of my routine when I was taking care of both my grandchildren when they were infants and toddlers was to take them once or twice a week to the grocery store. Many of the workers know them by their names and still ask about them every time I am there. I also love taking them to the bookstore to buy books. I remember when my grandson was two years old and we went to the book store, we started by playing with the train set and after he played with the trains I told him to choose some books to read in the store and then to choose a book to buy. He was capable of differentiating between the two, the books he wanted to read were not the same as the books he wanted to buy. It was a great adventure for him, and we used to go several times a month. People knew who he was and appreciated his desire for books, and it gave him a great sense of security and happiness, which made me happy as well. And today, this tradition goes on with my granddaughter and one of the things only the three of us do, without anybody else, is go to the bookstore to read books and purchase new ones.

Yael: It seems that you always have endless patience for us, even while shopping.

Sam: I loved going schlopping with you when you were young because it was a special time we shared together, just the two of us. Schlopping with my grandchildren is a way to create memories. I hope that the things I buy them and the experiences we share while shopping will linger on throughout their life.

Schlopping Tips

- Be gracious to salespeople.
- If you are on a limited budget, share this fact with your family. But don't put the responsibility on your children.
- Give your child a budget when you go shopping. They will benefit and learn to buy wisely.
- Paying it forward is a lesson kids will enjoy learning.
- At special events, it's ok to splurge in order to bring home priceless memorabilia.
- It's ok to be on the receiving end of generosity.
- Schlopping is about the relationships and memories we create.

8. The Final Schlopping List

"It's those memories that I want to hold on to."

Sheryl: The news came on a Thursday evening, soon after 7 p.m., shortly after the stores and travel agencies had closed, that Dad had taken a turn for the worse. Mom advised me to take a flight from Israel to America as soon as possible. This was back in 1984, and the only way to leave the country was to book a ticket with a travel agent. Sam and I went to our travel agent in the morning and I was able to book a flight for later that same afternoon. I quickly packed a few things in an oversized suitcase, knowing that any trip back to America also included shopping, and left for the airport. I was going alone

and leaving behind the support of my immediate family—
Sam, and my two children, Yotam and Yael, who were both
under the age of ten.

I had an overnight stopover in Amsterdam, a city that I had
never traveled to. I remembered that my dad had mentioned
that he had been there during World War II, but I knew little
more since he rarely spoke about his experience as an American soldier. He had a small Dutch wooden shoe, a souvenir
from his visit, one of the few trinkets he possessed. Arriv-
ing late in the evening, I took a train to the center of town,
and with a map in hand I started to search down the dimly lit
streets for my hotel. Not wanting to be too conspicuous, like a
lost person, I stopped every few blocks, under a streetlight, to
take a peek at my map in an attempt to locate the hotel where
I was staying. After walking around in circles several times,
past the red-light district where the "ladies of the night" sat
on windowsills in their sexy, revealing clothes advertising their
wares, I finally arrived at the hotel and collapsed. Since receiving the shocking call about Dad, all I could think about was
fear: fear of the unknown and fear surrounding the realization
that my father's condition was so severe that it could only be
a matter of time.

I thought, what would I do if something happens to him
before I get there? Although I was a thirty-three-year-old wife
and mother of two young children, I felt too young to lose my
father. I kept hoping that he would pull through and that perhaps my coming to visit would give him the strength to miraculously recover. I awoke the following morning and went for a

walk and had several hours to think. I just needed the fresh air, yet somehow I gravitated to the department stores. Here my father was gravely ill on the other side of the ocean and all I wanted to do was shop. Somehow it helped alleviate the terror that I was feeling, and I knew that I would need to find inner strength to support my mom and brothers without Sam and my children by my side. For some reason, I felt that had I gone to the Anne Frank House or to gaze at Van Gogh's paintings, thoughts of Dad would have haunted me, and I needed an outlet so I would stop thinking. Shopping is a way for me to achieve that mindless state. Walking through the rows, searching for an item to buy without having any purpose was a way to cope with the anxiety of waiting.

I do not remember exactly what I bought for the kids, most likely a wooden doll for Yael and a T-shirt for Yotam. But I do remember that when I got to the airport, I bought Dutch chocolate bars for Dad because he had always been a chocaholic, and for my Granddaddy Charlie I bought a package of Dutch tulips because I knew that with his love of flowers and his amazing green thumb he would be able to make them grow in his backyard garden among the pecan and live oak trees.

I arrived just in time to celebrate my father's sixty-fourth birthday, on the 28th of October. He was already in the state of *go-sais*, the Hebrew word for the state of being a person is when "in between worlds," lingering between life and death. Since he was in intensive care, we had to take turns sitting with him because no more than two people were allowed in the room at the same time. He went in and out of consciousness, waking up for several minutes and then dozing off.

This was really my first first-hand experience watching someone die. I had read about the stages of death, but here was my father, a sixty-four-year-old healthy man, who, due to a medical error (he had received an overdose of a prescribed medication for gout), had withered away and now we were slowly losing him. Over the course of the day, he would wake up intermittingly and touch his forehead, as if to check that he was still here on earth with us. He would mumble something, often incoherently, yet in his mind he was trying to say the things that he was thinking. I told him that I had been in Amsterdam on my way over, and he told me how he had loved visiting there when he was a soldier. We would chit-chat briefly, and then he would fall back to sleep. Once, he woke up and shook his hands in front of him and said, "Let me down slow and easy." He spoke as a man who was readying himself for death and trying to make sure we gently put him in the earth.

He was unable to eat, so we gave him Ensure shakes during the day to give him nourishment. I remember his comments and sense of satisfaction when we gave him a few sips on a spoon and he said how good it tasted, "Like vanilla milk shake." At one point I said that I was his daughter, Sheryl, and that if he heard me he should squeeze my hand. When he gave me a very strong squeeze, I felt such a feeling of warmth and satisfaction because I knew that my dad was aware that I was there next to him. He would come out with comments like,

"Take this picture and put it here and now put this one there," and I would say, "Ok, Dad, I did. Is there anything else you want me to do?" and his response was, "No, that's ok." Once, he woke up and said to me, "You need to make me laugh." I said to him, "You are the one who makes me laugh," and he replied, "Tell me a joke." I answered, "I can't tell jokes," and he said almost with a chuckle, "That's not good." Well, I was never good at jokes and always forget the punch lines, but I thought I should at least give it a try. I said, "Ok, I'll tell you a joke. A woman went into a supermarket…" But he stopped me in midsentence and said, "That's not the right one," and then dosed off again to sleep. Another time he awoke and said, "I don't want to play cards, I don't like to play cards," and I told him, "It's fine, you don't have to." He had always hated playing cards, so he just wanted to make sure that we weren't going to make him do that, even as a dying man. He was getting his life in order and somehow knew what was happening, even though none of us were willing to accept the inevitable.

I left the hospital late in the evening and other family members stayed through the night. Early the next morning, we received a phone call to come immediately. Upon arrival, we learned that he had gone into cardiac arrest. The doctors had done everything to revive him, but it was too late. My dearly beloved father, who had only two days previously celebrated his birthday, passed away peacefully in his sleep. When we got the news, I felt the room buzzing around me, the walls seemed to be falling in, and there was a numbness that overcame me with a feeling of emptiness that I had never before experienced. Everything was so sudden—his illness, his downturn, and now his death.

Dad's illness had begun two months prior and he had started to get his affairs in order. He prepared a hand-written list of specifics that he wanted at his funeral, based on traditional Jewish customs. He wanted to be buried in a traditional and modest way, so in keeping with the person he was. He requested to be buried in a simple pine box, with a closed casket and dressed with a white shroud with a *tallit*, the prayer shawl, and *yarmulke*, the skullcap that Jewish men wear. We chose the one I had crocheted for him for my wedding, twelve years prior.

Although the burial plot had been purchased, there were still so many arrangements we needed to make. Here we were in a relative state of shock having to make so many decisions. My older brother, Sam, and my younger brother, Harry, and I were the ones to step in and do the funeral planning. We went together to the funeral home and were presented with what was essentially a funeral-shopping menu. We had to make the choices that we felt would be suitable and respectable. We chose a few things from the menu, including ritual washing and purification of the body, and ongoing prayers to be said next to his body until the commencement of the services. It is customary that a person remain with the deceased at every moment until burial. We also needed to decide when and where the ceremony would take place, the newspapers in which to make the announcement (and until today some family members are angry that we did not choose the "right" newspaper), and how we would travel from the chapel to the family Jewish cemetery, which was two-and-a-half hours away. We chose to travel in our own cars instead of paying extra for a limousine, as Dad never would have wanted us to spend money on such frivolities.

We were very lucky because there was a consensus among us, whereas in some families these basic arrangements can cause such conflict. Never would I have thought that making final arrangements for our father's funeral would be a way for us siblings to share in this experience of choosing the best way to say our goodbye. If he were alive, he would have chuckled and laughed thinking that we went schlopping for his funeral.

Now, I needed to prepare for the funeral. After fifteen years of not living in America and no longer understanding its funeral etiquette, I was at a loss about what I needed to do. In Israel, a person who buries their loved one wears an old garment because following the burial ceremony, the shirt gets torn as a sign of mourning. Before leaving home, I packed a skirt and old black shirt, thinking that I could wear that if needed, only to be told that it was inappropriate funeral attire and I would need to buy something more respectful.

So my ex-sister-in-law and I went out schlopping. She was a person who never really cared about fashion and yet was there to help me find something suitable and appropriate to wear. Here my father had just passed away, and I was in the store rummaging through the racks of clothes looking for a complete outfit that would make me look as a mourning daughter should. Although it was almost thirty years ago, I vividly remember how my body felt—the buzzing and spinning in my head, the numbness in my body, and the disorientation resulting from knowing that here I was buying clothes and my father was cold and dead. She helped me in this pursuit, making recommendations, bringing in various items while I was in the dressing room trying on clothes and giving sisterly advice. We found the perfect two-piece outfit, a beautiful short-sleeve blouse made of black and gray tweed with a matching skirt and appropriate black shoes. There was also a beautiful matching long-sleeve, gray silk blouse that she insisted I buy since it fit me so well. All I could think about was that my father was dead and I had to worry that I was dressed appropriately. It was years before I could give away the shoes, and I did wear the outfit and blouse on special occasions. Although they no longer fit, they still remain hanging in the back of my closet. I cannot part with them because they remain special memories of my father.

The following spring, my grandfather sent me a picture of the multicolored tulips in full bloom in his garden. Not only did he love to grow flowers, but he also loved to take pictures of flowers, winning awards for both. When I received the photo by mail, three weeks after it was sent, tears swelled in my eyes as I remembered the shopping trip in the Amsterdam airport, the long flight over to America, and thinking about my father on his death bed. The memory of my father was blossoming in my grandparent's garden.

Schlopping in the Attic in Columbus

Sheryl: In 1997, when Gommie Clara was eighty-seven years old, she fell and was moved out of her home in Columbus, Texas, to a nursing home in Houston to be closer to her adult children. We, the family, had to clean out the house before it was sold, so I made a special trip to America to help my mom through this ordeal. This was the home where my mom had lived with her parents, along with her younger brother and sister, from the time she was a child, resulting in more than sixty years worth of accumulated things. Gommie Clara loved to entertain, and "the house in Columbus" was synonymous with gatherings of the immediate and extended families. We would congregate there for all the holidays and special events throughout the years.

Since my grandparents were in the clothing business and since Gommie loved to shop, the house was an extension of the store and looked like an antique department store. Downstairs was the kitchen with ceiling-high cabinets; the living room with a baby grand piano; the formal dining room with a samovar in the middle of the table; the family-room den with TV, reclining chair, shelves of toys and books, matchbook collections, and other miscellaneous items; my grandparents' bedroom with floor-to-ceiling sliding door mirrors; and the guest bedroom with the only air-conditioner in a bedroom.

On the second floor each child had their own bedroom, and even as their families expanded with grandchildren and then great-grandchildren, the upstairs rooms were still called by their names, "the Evelyn, Herb, and Maxine bedrooms." There were closets in every bedroom filled to the brim with old clothes, newspapers dating back decades, and, in my mom's closet, even a picture of Ronald Regan when he was an actor. Although my grandmother was a pack rat, she was very organized and each room had its own special collections. In one upstairs bedroom, there were hats of all shapes, fabrics, and colors, some with veils, flowers, sequins, or feathers. In another room, there were purses in every size, shape, and style, including fabric and leather clutches, hard plastic box bags, and crocheted and beaded bags. Inside almost every bag were monogrammed handkerchiefs and matching compacts and lipstick holders made of silver or gold to match the trim on the purses. There were separate drawers of gloves and wallets and costume jewelry. There were several old cedar chests with hand-crocheted and knitted quilts and duvet blanket covers that had not been used in years and smelled of the moth balls that had been placed inside for protection.

And then, of course, there was the attic. The attic was only partially finished, and as kids we were always told that we weren't allowed to go inside because it was dangerous and we could fall through the wooden slats. The attic is where my grandparents stored old letters dating back to the 1930s; boxes and boxes of ladies' shoes, that perhaps Gommie had once worn, or perhaps they were just overstocked from their store; endless boxes of photos and slides that Granddaddy had taken over the years, some of trips of faraway places and others of the flower shows that they had visited; and "my life." When I was eighteen years old and graduated high school and went to study abroad in Israel and never returned, my parents had moved to a smaller home and they "packed me up and moved me to the attic" at my grandparents' home. Over the years, when I returned to visit family, I would go to the attic and rummage through my belongings, including my personal collection of stuffed animals; ashtrays "borrowed" from restaurants during the 1960s; scrapbooks, including the one from the 1964 World's Fair in New York City, which showed a prototype of the microwave and a demonstration of the futuristic idea that you could see and talk to another person via the telephone line; an old, dried-up corsage from a junior high sock hop; a piece of Bazooka bubble gum, still in the original wrapper, from my first boyfriend; photo albums and correspondence with my high school buddies and flames; valentine cards; and so many other things that one collects over the years if you are a pack rat, as I am. Each trip back to America, I would return to Israel with a few more pieces of memorabilia from my childhood life in my suitcases, only to store them in closets or boxes in my home. Now there were important decisions to make about the future of all those things.

The schlopping that Mom and I had to do was not for new items, but rather involved going room by room to determine what to keep, what to sell, what to donate, and what to throw away. The house had been sold, and Gommie had already determined how to divide most of the important items among the various family members. Mom and I went to the house and had only three days to go through all the rooms. Some of the old clothes and hats were donated to the theatre department at the high school; letters that were written about activities of local community organizations were given to the municipal library; and so many other *tshatshkes*, trinkets or knickknacks, were left in the house to be put in an estate sale. Many local friends came to purchase small tokens from the home as a way to remember Charles and Clara Klein, who had been pillars in the community for decades, active in Rotary, the garden clubs, Masons, and Eastern Star, and founders of the local Jewish temple.

As we went through the piles of things, most of the special items that I wanted to keep had little monetary value. They were instead sentimental memories of life growing up in Columbus and the time I spent in the kitchen with Gommie, who loved to cook. These items included her extensive cookbook collection, a decades-old glass mixing bowl, two oversized stainless steel mixing spoons (one, which my grandchildren love to play with today, with slits used to skim the fat from chicken soup), and an apron that I had sewn as a teenager for Gommie. There was a teaspoon collection displayed in specially designed cabinets that had hung on the wall in the formal dining room and that represented the many places that they had visited in America and around the world. Another item was an antique bronze samovar that Louis Klein, my mother's paternal grandfather, had brought with him when he immigrated as a child to America from Europe in the late 1880s. That samovar has traveled for more than a century, across several oceans, from Europe, to New York, to Texas, to Israel, and now resides in Boston. My mom and I spent those wonderful three days together going room by room and schlopping among the memories of our lifetime as a way to keep the home in Columbus alive in our hearts.

Yael: Mourning periods are times to honor the dead and help the family and loved ones heal from the loss; they include sadness as well as memories of the joys their lives brought to the world. Laughter and sadness are universal, as are life and death. It is the way we deal with our emotions in social settings that connects us as well as divides us. Funeral arrangements and mourning customs vary among nations, religions, and cultures. What is acceptable in one country may be shunned in another.

At the end of 2013, the world experienced the loss of a great humanitarian and supporter of peace and equality, Nelson Mandela. A picture of three world leaders, President Barack Obama of the United States, Prime Minister Helle Thorning-Schmidt of Denmark, and Prime Minister David Cameron of the United Kingdom, taking a selfie showing their bright smiles and joyful eyes with a cell phone appeared in the media. Half the world was appalled and felt it was inappropriate and not proper etiquette at a memorial service. The photographer who was lucky enough to snap the picture of a lifetime declared that those who objected to the selfie did not understand the nature and ambience of the memorial service. He said that all around the stadium, South Africans were dancing, singing, and laughing to honor and celebrate their leader's life.

My first encounter with mourning customs in Tanzania occurred in 2013, when my son and I accompanied my professor dad, who was teaching his annual course on Economic Development of Tourism in Tanzania for Boston University. We were sitting in the hotel and suddenly heard men playing the drums and singing outside. I looked out the window to see an open truck carrying a dozen people, which my dad told me was a funeral. As a western woman, I was expecting the singing to be an artistic, joyful message, yet it was to inform the death of a loved one. Both a celebration of the man's life and the sadness of his death was being announced, two sides of the same coin of the universe.

I remembered my mom telling me about a Maasai woman she had interviewed while working in Tanzania who had lost her infant son an hour after the interview. On the ride back home, the woman was sitting on the floor of a vehicle, holding her infant child, when it flipped over, injuring her and killing her infant; it was horrific. My mom thought of her grandchildren safely seated in child seats while millions of people don't even have a seat at all to sit on in a car. My mom was going through her pictures that day and came across a picture of the woman and her infant. With tears, she went to show her Maasai translator the picture to ask how she could pass it to the grieving mother. He said, "Don't ever show that picture to her. Once a person dies, he dies, that's it. You don't talk about him." The following day, Mom went to the village to pay her respects, and the woman gave her several hand-beaded bracelets and refused to accept money from her. My mom purchased extra items as a way to support the family and gave her hand sanitizer, bandages, and gloves and showed her how to clean her wounds. Although the way we deal with mourning varies among the cultures and religions, the human feelings are the same.

In Judaism, the deceased is considered *tumah*, not pure, thus, burial should be done immediately after death, if possible within twenty-four hours, and in Israel, minimal preparation is required by the family. In Israel, there is the *Chevre Kadisha*, the National Burial Society, that takes care of all aspects of the funeral arrangements. They transport the body, preform purification rituals and dress the body in a religious shroud, pray continuously next to the body, and arrange the burial plot. The family usually does not have to worry about purchasing anything; all services are provided. Furthermore, the bodies go straight into the ground " you are dust, and to the dust you shall return." Thus, no arrangements for a coffin are needed. The family mourners wear old clothes and the shirt is torn following the burial as a sign of mourning. The clothing that is worn for the funeral is therefore ripped and often destroyed.

Friends and family are often notified only several hours prior to the funeral, so whatever the person is wearing is acceptable attire. Almost every man has a *yarmulke* in his car—as my Dad says, "Just in case he gets called for a funeral."

Mourners also participate in the burial and throw dirt to cover the body. Whether it is a handful or several shovels of dirt, everyone participates. After the burial, the family goes home to "sit *shivah*," which involves sitting for seven days at the family's home in order to pray and talk about the deceased. Mirrors are covered so that one does not worry about physical appearance and avoids vanity during the mourning period; the focus is on the loved one who has passed. Usually people who come to visit bring food and sometimes a catering service may be used. But other than food no preparations are required, no shopping rituals, just the opposite. It is not culturally acceptable to care for ones looks and purchase new items during the grieving period.

In 2013, Asaf and I went to our first wake in Boston for a friend. As we were getting dressed and he was choosing his tie and I was choosing my necklace, we looked at each other and felt strange; it was weird to "get pretty" to go to a funeral. When we got to the funeral home, we paid our respects to the family and saw there was an open casket. The casket bore a sticker showing the logo of the deceased's business, and the deceased was dressed in a hippy but respectful way, the way he dressed in life. After the ceremony, there was a gathering at the family home. As it happens everywhere in the world, people laughed and cried, shared memories, and sat solemnly. It was the same as what we were used to, nothing more nothing less. Same emotions, same celebration of life, same sadness at the loss—the only difference was that people were dressed more nicely and the deceased was in plain sight.

It is the balance of the culturally accepted rituals and our self-beliefs that allow us to grieve with love. Whether it is shopping in America for flowers and clothes, having a *yarmulke* in the car just in case, or singing and playing music on a truck, we all grieve and celebrate the lives of those we have lost with the same emotions.

It seems that terrorism is following me around everywhere, and no matter where I go I am still threatened by it every day and in every place. I have been in close proximity to seven terrorist attacks: four in Israel, two in America, and one in France. Why is it that we often keep memorabilia from sad and shocking events? I kept two metal bolts that flew onto my fourth-floor terrace from a terrorist bus bombing. The bus exploded underneath the entrance of my house in Tel Aviv; two dozen people lost their lives. I lived on Allenby Street, one of the main shopping streets, with restaurants, boutiques, public transportation, and people walking, driving, and cycling everywhere. I was at work and had just met a colleague who told me that her father was the owner of a falafel restaurant on Allenby, next to my home, that had been hit by a terrorist attack a couple of years before. After her father had healed from his injuries and the heart attack he had suffered as a result of the attack and the restaurant had been restored, he changed the name from Itzik's Falafel to The After Itzik's

Falafal to represent the reopening of the restaurant after the attack. Within ten minutes of this discussion, all the phones started to ring, and we saw on the news that a terrorist attack had taken place on Allenby again. We looked at each other horrified. We both left immediately, and when I entered my home I found policemen on my terrace guarding the street from above and accumulating debris important to an investigation. The debris was filled with nails and bolts that had been placed in the bomb in order to cause maximum harm to human beings. Some of the debris remained on the terrace after they left, and I saved a metal bolt in a special box. The neighbors got together and we all went downstairs to see how we could help and mourn together with the community. Within a few hours, after all the human parts were gathered, and the blood was washed away, the street reopened for business as usual. The biggest sensation I remember that still follows me to this day is the slaughterhouse smell that lingered on my home street.

On September 11, 2001, I was in New York City on my honeymoon, visiting Yotam, and watched the Twin Towers burn for days. I was sitting with the world watching on TV as one tower had fallen and the other was still standing and burning and couldn't believe my eyes. Thousands of people did what I call the American Terror Attack Walk. When a terrorist attack happens in America, the public transportation shuts down and tens of thousands of people are left stranded and forced to walk hour after hour to get to a safe place. We were waiting for our friend who was downtown at the time to take refuge with us in Queens. He walked for two-and-a-half hours in his business shoes and had blisters on his feet. On a regular day, the blisters would be a source of pain, but on that day they were a sign of survival. After a few hours when subway service began—Yotam, Asaf, and I decided to go into Manhattan to see the aftermath. It was horrific: white and gray debris was raining down on the city, covering dozens of blocks and making the air suffocating. For days, people were walking around in a daze, New Yorkers were telling strangers on the subway to be careful and to take care, and everybody was trying to help as much as they can.

After a terrorist attack, the way to survive and live our free lives is to continue our daily routine, go out to the streets, and stimulate the economy with shopping. When the streets came back to life, the first thing we did was to buy an "Osama Ben-Laden Wanted Dead or Alive" T-shirt from a street vendor. Even today, after I have worn and washed it hundreds of times, it is in the closet, and I will probably never get rid of it.

I was in Boston in April 2013 when the Boston Marathon terrorist attack hit and was shaken to my core. Five minutes before the bombs went off, I had been walking home with my kids after watching the marathon at Kenmore Square, one mile from the finish line. Again, tens of thousands of people did the American Terror Attack Walk—many of them, this time, in running shoes. Those running shoes became the symbol of the attack, often included in newspaper photos and in memorial monuments.

Four days after the terrorist attack, the police were on a manhunt. The city and its surrounding towns were shut down and my husband and I needed to drive to Tennessee for business. On the way, we passed by a shopping mall at midday on a Friday that was completely empty. It felt like a bad Christmas or Thanksgiving, where the stores were closed and all the radio stations were talking about the same issues with the same feelings. Only this time, it was with emotions of fear and sadness and the radio was playing solemn and patriotic songs as opposed to the celebratory music associated with a holiday.

We drove across America wearing our Boston Red Sox hoodies with sadness and pride. We were in Ohio when the radio announced the capture of the terrorists. For us, it was a moment of relief. It was amazing that the police and forces had found the terrorists within only four days; it made me feel safe. Both Osama bin Laden and the Boston terrorists had been caught and America had told the world that it would not back down to terrorism; if someone hurts us we will hunt you and capture you no matter how long it takes, whether four days or twelve years.

In Boston, a spontaneous, informal memorial site was set up in Copley Square. For weeks people visited and contributed flowers, shoes, letters, and pictures. People came together as one. After a few weeks and once the streets had opened, the memorial installation was moved to a different permanent location. The day Copley opened after the stores were rebuilt was a truly special day and people were encouraged to shop. Many did.

On the night the Red Sox won the 2013 World Series a few months later, we went to Fenway Park to celebrate with all. We witnessed the start of a spontaneous run that ended at the Boston Marathon finish line in Copley Square. That night, we wore our Boston Red Sox hoodies with double pride, and they now have an extra meaning when I see them in my closet. After the bombing in Boston, all I could think was: What does this mean about going out in public? Does it mean I will stop shopping in malls? Does it mean I will be too scared to continue our Fourth of July family tradition, going to the Esplanade to watch the fireworks? Does it mean I will be watching every person and every move when I'm out on the streets? Does it mean I will be frightened by public transportation, as I was from 2000 to 2004, when fifty suicide bus bombings took place in Israel and I refused to take public transportation? Does it mean I should fear for my child's safety because his daycare is one block from the terrorists' house? I thought I had left the frightening feeling of terrorism behind when I had left Israel. Never did I think it would follow me here to Boston.

So how do I cope with this new reality? The biggest difference this time around was that I was a parent. It was my responsibility to protect others and not just myself. But it is also my responsibility and privilege to live as a free person. I realized that giving in to terrorism while I live in America by changing my daily routine would act against the free country I live in. It was later revealed that the bombing had originally been planned to take place on the Fourth of July on the Esplanade. I had an internal countdown until July Fourth and was wondering if I would have the courage to take my kids to the Esplanade to celebrate the birth of America. When the day came, I could not *not* go. I felt that if I didn't go, I would have given in to terrorism. I therefore decided to continue to take our kids to public events, to continue my daily life, and to live with the knowledge that it might happen again. In a way, the Marathon bombing released me from the fear of terrorism, because terrorism can happen anywhere in the world, and so this particular act of terrorism taught me to live as I please.

After an attack, we try as a community to figure out what happened and to cope with the resulting loss and fear; together, we mourn and get through the wreckage. Whether it is greeting each other on the subway, playing solemn songs on the radio, starting a spontaneous run, or going on a shopping trip, we do what we can to remember and move on.

Was it sad to see this memorial spot go, or was it a good sign that life moves on and we continue on with our daily lives, incorporating the knowledge of what happened? What we keep and what we let go will vary for us socially, culturally, and with age. Am I saving the bolts and T-shirts to remind me of the events or to remind me of a period of history that I witnessed?

Dialogue between Sheryl and Yael, January, 2014

Yael: Mom, do you expect me to keep your outfit that you bought for your father's funeral? When will this piece of clothing be out of your closet? Or will it stay forever until it's my turn to go through the things in the attic? When is it too long to hang on to something?

Sheryl: When you put it that way, it sounds ridiculous that I kept it all these years. What is meaningful for one person has little or no meaning for another. I would want to pass on the wooden shoe from Amsterdam as opposed to the outfit. I would like you to inherit things that have a story behind them, such as memorabilia from places we traveled or gifts we received from others and then pass them on to the next generation.

Yael: What would you like us to do with all the things you have?

Sheryl: I guess you, Yotam, and your kids will have to determine the things you want. The reason I kept them was that they are part of my life. I am still holding on to knitted sweaters that my mom or mother-in-law knitted that are packed away; when I look at them they bring back wonderful memories. But you didn't even want to use the knitted things that were made for you as a baby for your babies. I guess I have an emotional connection to things.

Yael: Maybe the reason you keep the outfit is because you wore it the last time you were with your father physically. Maybe as long as you keep it, you still have the feeling that he is with you. And probably, for you, getting rid of the outfit would mean letting go of one more piece of him.

Sheryl: I think that if you want something to stay in the family to be passed on, it is important to find a way to make it meaningful to the next generation. You and Yotam used to laugh and fight about the samovar, always saying that the other one can have it. For me, it symbolized the migration of our family. It has moved with the family across oceans several times over more than 120 years. Growing up, it was on permanent display on the mantel in the dining room in Columbus and often used as a centerpiece for holiday parties. It's those memories that I want to hold on to.

What is important about all the things in our home—the pictures, the vases, the dolls, the pottery, the tea sets, the African ceremonial masks and wooden birthing stools, the Maasai jewelry and head pieces, and even the large kitchen spoons—is the story behind each one. These items were not acquired randomly or to show off elegance or status, but rather as a way to remember a person, a place, or a special trip. They often represent different time periods of my life.

Actually, when we were packing up and moving to Boston, you and Yotam were going through the house and already negotiating what each of you wanted or didn't want. Why did you choose those things? Why did you want the antique mirror that had been in the Louis and Raye Klein store and then was passed down to Gommie and Granddaddy and then to Savta Evelyn? Why was that important to you? Your daughter loves to play with the elephant that you got when you were an infant from Gommie Mildred, my dad's mother; will she want to keep that? Your son loves to play with the Lego that you and Yotam had as children; will he want other things as memories of Savta and Saba's home? Your daughter loves putting on the apron, which she calls her gown, that was your Savta Eva's, your dad's mother, who passed away almost thirty years ago. When she wears it, you explain to her the origin of her name and the relationships of her ancestry; will she want to keep that? Both of them love taking the large metal spoons that came from Gommie's kitchen and digging with them for dinosaur bones while they play paleontologist with paper towels and dinosaur toys; will they want to keep them? Will you want to keep all those things to pass on to your children? Although the meaning may differ for each of us, I hope that there will be some things from our home that you will want to keep for you and your children and future generations. It might be a silver tray, or a hand-sewn apron fraying at the seams, or the African masks, or the samovar, but you will have to determine what is meaningful for you in your life.

Schlopping Tips

- To ease the pain of your loved ones, try to make specific arrangements for when you pass away so that they do not need to decide or fight during these confusing times.
- When making the arrangements, be respectful of your family members. Do not make a crazy request unless you are sure it will be received with humor.
- Make sure you have a current estate plan and will.
- You can also make an "ethical will," which is special notes to your family about the objects you are leaving or lessons you have learned through life. These will be cherished.
- Try to be socially appropriate while being true to yourself.
- If you see a person dressed or behaving outside the norm, it does not mean they are disrespectful.
- When deciding what to keep and what to throw away, follow your heart and think of the past and future generations.
- If you wish to impart special meaning to some object, use it on a daily basis or on special events with the younger generation. Do not keep it closed up in the closet.

9. Is There A Schlopping Gene?

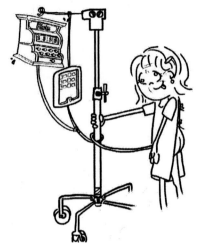

"There is something about walking the aisles and looking, even if I don't buy, or even if I buy only a tube of toothpaste, that gives me such satisfaction."

WHY IS IT THAT SOME PEOPLE LOVE SHOPPING so much, yet others cringe at the thought of it? What is the rush that makes people shopping addicts, or shopoholics? Is it the decision-making process, the feelings resulting from acquiring new items, the monetary aspect, the communication with others while shopping? Or is it the comfort one gets from being among all the new things? Are we born addicted to shopping, or do we acquire the habit as we go through life?

There are various reasons why people shop: to purchase basic needs such as food and clothes; to replace a broken item or upgrade a new gadget; to reward oneself or others for a job well done, a promotion, or after an illness; to purchase special items for special events, such as weddings, births, and funerals; to gather information about the products we may wish to purchase by comparing them with others; and to have some time away from the house, either alone or with others. And then there are people who shop to fill an emotional vacuum or to satisfy an addiction.

The way we shop varies among the generations as well. The Great Depression generation bought something for life and kept it. They used to put plastic covers on their couches in order to keep them fresh and clean and often went shopping for new items only when the old items broke and were beyond repair. Baby boomers have more money than their parents had, more opportunities to buy, and more technology that makes it easier to buy almost anything. They buy a lot and keep a lot and often have dozens of extra items "just in case." They seldom throw away their belongings, thinking they should keep them for their kids and grandkids or "because you never know when I might need this." Items that do not fall into one of these two categories are donated to charity. Generation X and Generation Y buy and throw out. They are used to having so much stuff that throwing away, giving away, or selling their belongings are part of their daily life. They buy dozens of socks, and if one has a hole in it they will throw the pair away and buy a new one as opposed to darning. They are also technologically savvy and view having the latest version of technology and upgrading as necessities of life. Shopping for apps and games for computers and phones is part of their daily shopping. When new phones or games hit the market, people wait in line for hours just to be the first to have the new, upgraded version of technology. What the boomers, Gen Xers, and Gen Yers will teach Generation i, as well as the changing times, will determine the future of shopping and shopping addiction.

Shopping has changed: we are no longer restricted to shopping in stores; we can also shop online by ourselves and try to get the best possible deal. Comparing prices, researching the pros and cons of merchandise, and reading other people's reviews on the internet are now a part of our shopping routine. We often spend hours, days, and even months on the computer before we purchase an item to make sure that our decision-making process includes the best information we can gather.

Gender attitudes about shopping have also changed. The men in the Great Depression and baby boom generations often hated shopping and shopped only when absolutely necessary. Many viewed it as a "womanly thing" that is a waste of time. However, Generation-X, -Y, and -i men and male children have no shame about shopping—in fact, just the opposite. Many love shopping; shop with their parents, spouses, significant others, and friends; and take pride in their love of shopping. Some are addicted to it from an early age.

Where we buy things has also changed with time and varies among generations. Buying in second-hand stores used to be stigmatized as something only lower-class people did, and middle- and upper-class people would never be seen in those stores. But today, it is just considered frugal or even ecological. Although most middle-class baby boomers never shopped at the Salvation Army, they did go to garage sales, as it was part of being a member of a community. Today, second-hand stores, garage sales, and Freecycle are all part of the culture of shopping and are no longer considered shameful. In fact, many people take pride in finding a "great bargain" through these venues—and will tweet about their accomplishment.

The shopping addiction used to involve going into stores, roaming the aisles, talking to people, and purchasing new items at the cash register. It has evolved into looking on your phone to compare products and prices, reading other people's reviews, and purchasing items by tapping a screen. Generations X, Y, and i as well as baby boomers are now addicted to social networking, being connected to the web 24/7, and using smart phones while they shop. Solicitation and bargain emails have emerged, and people are shopping much more frequently than they used to because the "shop" is now at their fingertips. The feeling of the screen tap has become just as addictive as the sound of the cash register ringing.

Although online shopping has taken the interpersonal relationships with schlopping buddies, salespeople, and fellow shoppers out of the shopping experience, smart phones can now connect people in shared shopping experiences even when they are not physically together. The dressing room is now global as shoppers send pictures to their friends via social media to help them decide what to buy. Only time will tell if it will come true, but one new forecast is that you will soon be able to take any person, dead or alive, with you as a virtual reality schlopping buddy.

Many have researched shopaholics and their addiction. We have defined Shopaholic Symptoms and Behaviors (SSB). These include:

1. purchasing things every day, even if it is just a candy bar, bread, or milk;
2. having numerous unopened items or garments with tags still attached in the closet;
3. purchasing unnecessary items;
4. shopping beyond one's means;
5. going shopping when angry or to relieve stress;
6. feeling a rush, a high, or security while shopping;
7. feeling remorse and guilt after shopping;
8. hiding one's purchases from others;
9. feeling withdrawal and anxiety on days one doesn't shop; and
10. rationalizing every purchase.

We two are very different. Sheryl is a compulsive shopper and has all the symptoms and behaviors of a shopaholic, while Yael is not. Is this due to nature or nurture?

Excerpts from Sheryl's journals and messages that show examples of SSBs

Journal: June 12, 2003
{SSB: 1, 3, 4, 6, 10}

I don't know what the problem is with me; I really am a compulsive shopper. It's not that I go out and buy large, expensive items in one shot—not expensive jewelry or furniture or appliances or gadgets. It's just that it seems I have to always be buying {SSB #1 Purchasing things every day}. The odd thing is that I can account for almost every penny if I really try, and when it is divided up, it just doesn't seem too much. I somehow need these things around me. Why did I have to go overboard at the clown conference {SSB #3 Unnecessary items}? Part of it was for the kids, and they did use some of it for Purim {SSB # 10 Rationalize}. But all the clowning stuff?? I get all excited about things and then come back to reality {SSB #6 Feeling a rush}. . . . Does it give me the sense of security that we now have money? . . . There were years of not buying anything, no clothes, nothing for the kids. Yet it seems that when I would return to America, I would also buy with money that we didn't have, whether it was toys or clothes for the kids {SSB #4 Beyond your means}.

Why do I have so much junk and clutter? Why do I continue to collect? Even now, when I was trying to get rid of clothes, I bought a whole new closetful. Part of the clothes issue is the fact that for the first time in a very, very long time, I feel that I am wearing clothes well. . . . I think most of the clothes I bought are really nice things. I feel good in them and I feel that they make me look good. . . . So why the books????? On one hand, I feel that I want to minimize and on the other I continue to buy and buy and buy. Even the books—it's like a security blanket. I think I bought every book in the used-book store that looked relevant in any way to women's health, a lot on mothers-daughters, for my Ph.D. And many of the books have references to other books, which takes me down the detective trail of searching for more and more references. I just cleared off a lot of shelves and promised myself not to accumulate more. But what have I done? Bought more of them. I just need more room now, and to buy more shelves for books!!!!

Email message sent to Sam while he was in Liberia: October 11, 2008 {SSB: 2, 10}

Hey there,

I hit the jackpot today. Actually, I wish I had hit the lottery, but not yet. I went out this evening for a walk and went into Lord & Taylor, which was not my idea for a destination, but that is where I somehow ended up. Something great has happened to my body recently: I have actually been able to get into clothes that I haven't been able to wear for a couple of years. Sam, I finally found some great clothes at L&T that really look great!!! Pants in 10P and jeans that really make me look hot and sexy!!!! And what's even better is that the woman said to call her after October 23 and everything should not only be on sale but she will give me another "friends and family" coupon so all will be almost 50 percent off of the original price!!!! I'm just hanging them in the closet and waiting {SSB #2 Unopened items in Closet}. The reason to buy now is that they had my size, which doesn't always happen {SSB #10 Rationalize}. I just can't wait to start to work and have a reason to dress nicely again in my new job! I have actually missed that. I remember when I got the job at the Ben-Gurion University Overseas Program and I had to buy clothes for the first trip to America (they all still fit me great) and I felt like a million dollars. I also kept dressing like that in Israel as well and realized that I just missed it. There was never a reason here to put on anything nice: sitting behind a cubicle all day, it never made sense. I guess better clothes really do look nice on me, and they were not that expensive, even at full price. But when they go on sale, they will even be better. I have enough to go through the winter with great things. You can't imagine how wonderful it is to go to a store and find both pants and tops that really look great on me. Now that I am "even," it's so much fun to shop!!! For the first time in many, many years I feel that I can allow myself to buy a few things and just not feel guilty. A few different outfits that match each other can go a long way.

Journal: December 29, 2012 {SSB: 1, 5, 6, 9}

I am addicted to shopping. The same thing happened when

Yael and I were in Warwick on Christmas Eve. The location was horrendous. The only reason we went that direction was that we were planning to spend Christmas day with Yotam. However, to my delight, it turned out that we were about three minutes from a Stop&Shop and about five minutes from a mall that had a Target and a Macy's. We were working on our book, and the clock was ticking until the stores would close for the twenty-four-hour Christmas holiday break from retail . . . so I ran back to Target to get just a few things that we would need when the stores were closed, such as additional pens, Post-its, a baby toilet seat, etc., and then on to Macy's to get a few last-minute gifts, that in the end I am returning. I had the feeling of OMG, the stores will be closed and I won't be able to shop {SSB #9 Anxiety on days you don't shop}.

The same thing has happened this weekend. We are now in Portsmouth, NH, at a Homewood Suites. We have a king-size bedroom with a door that closes. I couldn't sleep in the middle of the night, being stuffed up from a bad cold. All I wanted to do was get in the car first thing in the morning and go home to my own bed. So I started checking out the stores online and found a Target about ten minutes away. . . . I came totally unprepared for this trip, I'm freezing in this room, I didn't bring any heavy clothes, and I'm just feeling bad. So I figured I would find a Macy's. When I went into their site, the closest seemed to be on the North Shore, between here and Boston. But then I put my Sheryl Smarts into action and looked up a JCPenney, and, lo and behold, I found a Simon Mall about five minutes away!!! Somehow, that has made me feel great, and I have planned to stay through the weekend {SSB #5 To relieve stress}. Just a few minutes ago, I was grieving about wasting money on a room and food, and now I am in seventh heaven thinking that I can spend more in the mall! Am I crazy? What is it that makes me want to shop? As I told Mom yesterday, I get shopping withdrawal if I don't buy something or go into a store every day, even if it's just a CVS or supermarket {SSB #1 Purchasing things every day}. There is something about walking the aisles and looking, even if I don't buy, or even if I buy only a tube of toothpaste, that gives me such satisfaction. Perhaps it takes me back to my childhood. In fact, I can picture myself a young girl of perhaps six or seven in Columbus when Gommie gave me a quarter, or perhaps I had earned it by making the bows that get put on the boxes for gift wrapping . . . and I would go into the 5 & 10 cent store. . . . I would go in and walk the aisles, around and around, looking to see what I wanted to buy, checking the prices and trying to figure out what and how much I could buy with my quarter. Most of the time, I would return to The Store, as we called Gommie and Granddaddy's store, empty handed but richer that day by a quarter. I was always one to save, thinking that if I kept my money this week, I would have more to spend the next time. I vividly remember once buying Mom perfume only to feel very upset when I gave it to her and she never wore it. Little did I know that perfume from the corner 5 & 10 cent store wasn't exactly what she wanted to wear. Was it the walking around the aisles, looking at the displays, seeing the variety of merchandize, the toys and all the other items that I enjoyed? I am not sure what it is, but even today, as I have come to middle age—actually, I guess you could say I've already passed that milestone—I still get a wonderful, warm feeling of security as I roam around aisles in stores {SSB #6 Feeling a rush}.

So here I am, on a getaway weekend with Sam . . . and I am ecstatic that instead of having a quiet romantic weekend with hubby, I am already dreaming of shopping in a few hours when the stores open {SSB #6 Feeling a rush}. I think that there really is a shopping gene, and I am certain that I have inherited it from my grandmother and mother and hope to pass on to the next generations.

Just looking at the list of stores, there is a Macy's, JCPenney, and Sears, so I can return all the gifts and perhaps get Sam out shopping to buy a few new clothes, since he walks around looking like a schlumpy, homeless aging hippie, with his beard, balding head, and pot belly, and ragged, torn clothes, and dirty tennis shoes. Perhaps we can spend some time together getting him a few new things!

Sheryl: I have all the Shopaholic Symptoms and Behaviors. I buy things every day, even if it is just milk or toothpaste; I get itchy if I don't shop for a few days; I rationalize every purchase I make; I pamper myself with shopping after every dentist or medical procedure; I feel happy and secure when I shop; I often regret what I buy; and I always have a bag of garments with the tags on them waiting to be returned. Although I no longer hide my purchases or feel guilty about them, there were many times over the years that I did. {SSB #7 Feeling remorse and guilt, SSB #8 Hiding purchases}.

When I try to think back over my life to remember when I first realized that perhaps my addiction resulted from an inherited gene, it takes me back many years to when I was very young. From as long ago as I can remember, I loved shopping with my mom. This was a special time for the two of us, without my brothers or my dad, where she and I could have time alone. Even with all the conflicts that may have existed when I was younger, or our very different body types that may have caused difference of opinions in the dressing room, our time together over the many decades has been a way of life that I always cherish. When I was young, we mostly shopped for special occasions, and then, as the years went by, it just became a way of life for us to spend mom-and-daughter time together.

From a very young age, every visit to our grandparents included the Sunday schlopping trip to The Store, when all the women would go to buy—that is, take things—from the store. On one of these trips when we were teenagers, Gommie told my cousin Lisa and me to make a list of every item that we took from the store and then calculate the total retail value. To say the least, we were shocked when we realized that we had just been given hundreds of dollars worth of clothes and we both learned a very important lesson about the value of money. To this day, we both have fond memories of those times together spent schlopping in the store. My grandparents always just gave us anything we wanted and we were never asked to pay, as that was their way to give presents to their family. In fact, when my paternal grandmother came from New York once to visit us in Texas and she went to the store and found something to buy, I told her, "You don't have to pay; you just take whatever you want." Of course she did pay, but only the wholesale price. When I was about ten or eleven, I got my first job in their store, along with Lisa. We learned how to make bows on a manual bow-making machine and to properly wrap gift boxes for the holiday season. We earned a penny for each bow, and, often, at the end of our workday, our grandparents gave us an extra fifty-cents bonus for our hard work.

My grandparents went to "market" twice a year, once in Dallas and once in Houston, to the wholesale showrooms to view the new styles and different brands of clothes. I remember going on several trips with them as a teenager. There were racks and racks of the latest designs and my grandparents, mostly my grandmother, had to choose the items that she thought would sell in their store. She thought not only of her long-term local clients, but also of all the women in the family. As we went from one showroom to another, she would say to my grandfather, "This will look good on Evelyn, and this one on Maxine, Lolly, Lisa, and Sheryl." My grandfather's response, so typical of men, was, "So what will be left in the store to sell?" Gommie always won.

I was really lucky in those days because the display sizes were very small, so I was able not only to try on the clothes in the showrooms, but also to take them home with me at the end of the day! These trips with my grandparents to market were so special; there was something magical about seeing so many styles and colors and designs. The atmosphere was somehow different from going into a retail store. Although I spent a lot of time at my grandparents' store, market was different. They always went with several of my great-uncles and their wives, who had their own Klein's stores in neighboring towns in Texas. I loved being the center of attention of all those older relatives. Although the stores were all independently owned and never became Neiman Marcus or Bloomingdale's, their fame came in other ways. The brothers went to market together and often exchanged merchandise at family functions. While looking at the clothes, they spoke in a code language about how much they wanted to pay wholesale and what they thought their retail price would be, already thinking of their profit margins. This language consisted of combinations of letters that made no sense to an outsider, such as LSX. These code letters were always written below the actual retail price on every tag on all items in their store. My parents also used this code when discussing all financial matters, such as when buying a car or discussing the amount of money my dad had made on his daily commission at work. Those financial matters were never something to be discussed around kids, so this was their secret language. For years, we asked what it meant and were always told we were too young to understand. My mother finally divulged the family secret only a few years ago.

I left home right after completing high school at the age of eighteen and moved across the ocean to Israel. Schlopping with my mom took on a different meaning since it was no longer something we could do on a regular basis. With every family visit, we took advantage of our time together, and shopping was always an important way to make up for lost time.

My dad worked in retail all his adult life. He was the owner of a dry-goods store in the small Texas town where we lived until I was two years old. After we moved to Houston, he worked in managerial positions in a large, upscale department store. Although he was always impeccably dressed in suit and tie for work, as soon as he arrived home he changed into shorts and T-shirts. We never really went shopping together for my clothes, yet from the age of fifteen I worked as a cashier in the department store where he worked and clothes and merchandise were always dinner-table conversation. He spent his entire adult life selling clothes, and schlopping was in his blood. I truly believe that there is a schlopping gene that has been passed down from my ancestors over the many generations of store owners and merchants and salespeople in our family.

Several years ago, I taught a class called The Sociology of Women's Health for incarcerated women who were studying for their bachelor's degree from Boston University. One day, I arrived at the prison the same day a former student of mine was being released after serving a seven-year sentence. When I asked her what she planned to do as a free woman, she replied, "The first thing I want to do is to go shopping."

A year and a half ago, I was driving home from visiting my mother and saw a big sign that said, "Marshalls coming soon." I ran into the house bursting with excitement, screaming with joy like a teenager, and felt an overwhelming sense of satisfaction that one of my favorite stores would be within a five-minute walk from home. I anxiously waited months for opening day and woke up early in the morning in order to arrive before 7 a.m., when the doors first opened. I felt a rush of energy and excitement to be one of the first customers to enter this new store and literally was jumping for joy! I bought clothes and toys for the grandchildren and piled them in the living room so when they woke up they would see the new purchases. Since we have been living together temporarily as a multigenerational family, we have all enjoyed evening strolls down the block to just look to see what they have; it's hit or miss, because one never knows what clothes, toys, or shoes will be in Marshalls on any given day. Perhaps that is part of the fun, finding an item that was unexpected but nevertheless something that is needed. As happy as I was when I heard they were opening, I felt that same sadness just a few weeks ago when I went into the store to buy winter clothes for the kids and was shocked to see that the entire section of kids' clothes and toys had disappeared overnight. I ran to the nearest salesperson to inquire where they had been moved, only to find out that this store would no longer carry kids' items. I had to break this disappointing news to my grandchildren, who were also very saddened. But they just said, "Savta, we can go to another Marshalls or to Target to buy clothes and toys."

I truly believe (with apologies to Sam, my husband, who is a geneticist) that I have passed on this gene to them, and I hope that they will always love to schlop and will always think of their "Savta schlopping trips" as wonderful memories of their childhood.

Yael: I have a love-hate relationship with shopping. I love shopping, and some of the best times in my life have been shopping with my mom. When we were shopping, my mom always used to give me a sense of security by letting me know that I could buy anything within reason. She also used to dote on me and compliment me all the time. I felt I was getting pampered by everybody, my mom and the salespeople, and often I got a little high and a rush when people would make a fuss over me while I was shopping. It was as if everybody was there to take care of my needs and make me look pretty, which made me feel like the most beautiful girl in the world.

On the other hand, I never had money growing up and even as a young adult always struggled as a student or new professional and hated the thought of wasting money. Like my dad, I calculated every single item and its price in order to decide whether it was worth buying or not. I also often felt guilty for taking money from my parents or for having them spend money on purchases for me, and so I often viewed shopping as a waste of money. I remember once, when I was fourteen years old and went bra-schlopping with Mom—probably our first time together bra-schlopping—and I refused to buy a bra because it was too expensive. My mom told me that there are two things you should always spend enough money on to buy good quality: bras and shoes. Only after some convincing from my mom did I agree to buy the more expensive bra.

Often, too, my mom had a way of making sure that I bought what she wanted and not what she did not want. She would either forget the item or say it was cheaper in a different store or that it was made poorly. But the amount of money she spent on things varied depending on whether she wanted to purchase them or not. I therefore felt growing up that shopping wasn't really about only my decision or under my control.

I loved shopping with my mom but did not like window shopping with her. While we would walk around the streets and look at fancy clothes in high-end stores, she would always say, "That would look so beautiful on you. One day when you have money, you can buy it." That always made me feel as if I would never have enough money and those clothes were out of reach.

Although it is true, as my mom always says, that from a young age I knew what I wanted and went for it, it is often difficult for me to decide. I remember spending over an hour and a half trying to decide if I should buy a jacket in medium or small. I guess the deliberation was also due to the fact that I was three months pregnant and didn't know which size I would need once my body was back to "normal."

After my son was born and I was a law student, money was very tight. I got addicted to Freecycle, which is an internet group that allows people to trade things for free. I used to check it daily to see if I could find toys and other household items. I brought home dozens of things, such as a plastic cashier register, a little piano, a toy lawn mower, a toy car, a dining room table, and various other items that often we did not need. After about eight months of doing this on a daily basis and accumulating too many things, I had to stop. I told my mom I was going to throw a lot of the things out, and she said, typical of a baby boomer, "Just give them to me and I'll put them in storage just in case we need them."

My mom has difficulties parting with things, and when I say I want to throw something out she gets very offensive and says, "With you, it's always throw away, throw everything out. You have no respect for things. You never know if you will need to use it. Give it to me, I'll save it for when we need it." It is *crazy*. I feel she doesn't understand my generation, which views items as objects to be used and not to be kept and saved forever. However, I do feel that I have "inherited" my mom's attachment to things and often accumulate so much stuff that it is as if things are controlling me and not the other way around.

My children love to shop. My son can go to a store for hours just going through shelves in order to choose the right toy. Often it will be the first one he picks or the smallest and cheapest item, but it is an item that he likes and that makes him feel secure. He will say, "Let's go on Amazon and order a book or toy and then wait for the truck to deliver it." I asked my son what he likes about shopping, and he said, "Choosing the toy and bringing the toy home to play with." It is as if it is in his blood to go to a store and shop for things he loves. I guess this is another personality trait that skips a generation.

Is the love for shopping inherited through genes or is it passed from one generation to the next due to the positive experiences a child has with his parents while shopping? I love the rush I get from shopping with my mom, and my son often prefers to go shopping over any other activity in the world. Is my son a product of his grandmother due to their shared nature or shared nurture?

Schlopping Tips

- It's ok to be addicted to schlopping, as long as it does not overly consume you financially or emotionally.
- If you are family of schloppers incorporate strategies that help you create positive experiences.
- If you have family members who are addicted to schlopping and it is harming them, confront them and try to reason with them.
- When schlopping is too time consuming or is taking away from relationships and success, take a hiatus.
- Have fun with schlopping, but remember it is a tool in life, not a goal.

10. Trust Your Schlopping Buddy From Ages 2 to 82

**"You can never be in someone else's shoes.
So if they say the shoe fits, let them wear it."**

WHEN ONE SHOPS for or with a schlopping buddy who is a child or an elderly or disabled person, there may be conflicts concerning who makes the decisions about what to buy. When we are children, our parents or grandparents are usually the people who make the decision. As the decades pass, often there is a reversal of roles, and the grown-up children will decide for their elderly parent. No matter what decade you are in, and what role you play, it is important to listen to your schlopping buddy.

Sheryl, age 8, in the 1950s

Sheryl: The family legend passed down through the generations is that my great-grandparents, Louis and Raye Klein, sold sexy bras, negligées, and lingerie to the "ladies of the night" who worked at the Chicken Ranch in La Grange, Texas. The story of the Chicken Ranch was adapted into the hit Broadway show and later the movie *The Best Little Whore House in Texas*, and some say, true or false, that in the Broadway play there was a large painted sign on a backdrop curtain that said "Klein's."

During the Great Depression, many men had limited finances and could not spare their money for their night's pleasure. Thus, "a chicken for a lay" policy was issued so that the brothel could keep its doors open. The women used the chickens for food and sold their eggs and poultry to supplement their income. It has been said that the local sheriff visited or called the Chicken Ranch every night to find out if any of the patrons had bragged to the ladies about their illegal activities and that as a result many crimes were solved.

My great-grandparents were married in 1901, lived in La Grange, Texas, had one daughter and six sons, and owned a small dry-goods store. Due to economic difficulties in Texas, they moved to the east coast for several years in the early 1920s, and it has been said that Raye opened the first corset department in Macy's in New York City and that Louis designed ladies lingerie: perhaps this was his way to learn about the needs of his local clientele. Raye often traveled by train back to New York City to buy specialty items that were unavailable at that time in Texas, such as ready-made bras. Many men on the way to the Chicken Ranch often stopped at the Klein's store in Schulenburg, owned by my great-uncle Myke, to buy the ladies special gifts for their visits.

When I was about eight years old, Gommie and I went to Louis's store in order to buy a pair of shoes. My one memory was that the shoes he fitted me with were at least one or two sizes too big. When I told this to Gommie, her comment was, "Granddaddy Klein sold everyone, especially kids, shoes that were a little too big, since this way, you would have room to grow." Although the shoes didn't fit right, I eventually grew into them and they lasted for several years. I wonder if he fitted the ladies a size larger as well.

The story goes that when the Chicken Ranch closed in the 1970s, the sales at the store in La Grange plummeted so severely that eventually the store was forced to close its doors. I guess the women, the men, and the Klein's suffered equally from the loss of the The Best Little Whore House in Texas. What a legacy to think that my ancestors' stores were a great success due to satisfying the shopping needs of these "ladies of the night."

Sheryl, age 10, in the 1960s

Sheryl: I always had flat feet and when I was a child, the myth was that if you wore shoes with good support somehow your foot would miraculously mold around the arch, resulting in the loss of the "flatfootedness." My mom, feeling that she was doing me a great service and being a very caring and loving parent, decided I needed to wear black and white saddle oxfords with specially made inserts to go along with knee high socks and poodle skirts.

Even with all my verbal and nonverbal protests—including screaming, yelling, and slamming the door—Mom would not budge and not only bought me those hideous, clunky shoes, but also made me wear them to school every day. In those days, the dress codes at school banned tennis shoes and sandals and allowed only closed shoes such as pumps or saddle oxfords. Kids at school made fun of me for wearing these shoes and having hairy legs. Mom said that I would have to wear them until I wore them out or outgrew them.

I did anything and everything to destroy them, including deliberately walking through puddles and scuffing them against rocks so that I would no longer have to wear them. After about six months, I finally won my battle and was able to get a nicer pair of shoes. My mom made the decision for me because she felt I was too young to decide and the shoes would improve my arches. After I successfully destroyed them, Mom finally understood my dismay about these shoes and never made me wear them again.

Yael, age 2, in the 1970s

Sheryl: From a very young age, Yael knew exactly what she wanted, what clothes she liked and what shoes she liked, and this was not always easy for the parent of a toddler. Each morning before going to nursery school, she stood in front of her closet and picked out her own clothes. There were days she wanted only to wear dresses and other days she wanted only shorts and T-shirts. Some days she wanted a long ponytail and other days two long braids.

Her choices were often influenced by her friends at nursery school or pictures of girls in books we read. For example, in one of her favorite books, the girl wore dresses and tennis shoes, so Yael decided at the age of two that she would wear only tennis shoes, not cutesy little girly shoes with her dresses. Her choice in shoes and clothes was already a way that she was expressing her independence, her decisiveness, and her strong will.

In those days I sewed clothes and made us matching shift dresses, with red, white, and blue stripes from fabric that was soft on the skin for the warm summer days. Actually, the matching dresses were for three of us, Yael, her doll, and me. Yael would carry the doll around endlessly, as she and her doll wore identical dresses. Yael loved this dress and as soon as she put it on she wanted to wear it day in and day out for about two weeks. So every evening after she came home from nursery school, I hand washed the dress, hung it to dry, and then it was back on her the following morning. I guess in some ways it alleviated the "what will I wear" daily saga. I remember the need to explain to her teacher, almost out of embarrassment, that Yael was so persistent and wanted to wear it every day. Yet the dress was clean each morning.

The schlopping trip that Yael and I went on was to the center of town to the local shoe stores. We went into a store and Yael picked out some shoes to try on. She knew which ones she liked by looking at the shelves with the shoes. When she started to try on a pair, I vividly remember, as if it were today although it was over thirty years ago, that she said, "Mommy, they don't feel good." When the salesman heard this, his comment was, "What does a child this age know? They look nice."

I explained to him that if she says that they are uncomfortable, then they are uncomfortable! On that note, we left the store. I didn't need some middle-aged shoe salesman, Al Bundy type, trying to convince me that the shoes that my two-year-old daughter said were not comfortable were a good fit. He wasn't the one who would have to wear them. We found another store down the street and continued trying on shoes until we found a pair that Yael liked.

Yael, age 10, in the 1980s

Sheryl: When Yael was ten, we lived in Beer Sheva, a relatively small town with limited shopping, since the malls had not yet been built. Therefore, periodically, on vacation days from school, Yael and I went on schlopping trips to the "big city," Tel Aviv, which was an hour and a half away. We would wake up early in the morning, take a bus, and arrive at the central bus station and begin our day. This particular trip, we had a mission: she needed new tennis shoes and, with the winter approaching, warm house slippers for the cold stone floors.

We spent the day going to the various open-air markets for inexpensive clothes for the upcoming cold weather, and found a few toys, books, and, of course, shoes. Yael's foot was smaller than mine yet was rapidly growing and she needed new tennis shoes almost every three to four months. At that time, tennis shoes were very expensive in Israel, and after trying on various shoes, she wanted a particular pair that cost fifty dollars. I just didn't want to spend so much money on a pair of shoes that would last only a few months.

The crazy idea that kept going through my mind was, if Yael were wearing the same size as me, I would be willing to spend more money, so that when she grew out of them I would be able to wear her "hand me ups." I was so embarrassed to even think such a thought that I never, until this time, disclosed what I was really thinking as we schlopped that day for shoes.

Although I chose not to buy her new tennis shoes, we finally found some nice warm slippers that fit and were inexpensive. There was only one problem that day: it started to rain and pour and Yael ended up walking around for over an hour in soaking wet shoes. Her only salvation was that when we finally got on the bus late in the afternoon for our return trip home, she was able to put on her new, dry slippers to keep her feet warm and snuggly.

Yael, age 12, in the 1990s

Sheryl: We had just completed a year of sabbatical in Tucson, Arizona, and were in Houston, Texas, visiting with my mom, on our way back home to Israel. Mom, Yael, and I went to a large department store and stumbled across a great sale for suede winter boots. By this time, Yael was in a size 7, a size larger than mine, and they were on sale, so she started trying them on with the intent to buy.

The salesperson kept going back and forth to the storage room bringing out stacks and stacks of boxes, boots in red and gold and black and blue and green. There were so many colors that it was almost impossible to decide which one to buy. Being the spendthrift that I am, I insisted that since they were such a great bargain and I was convinced that her feet had now reached their adult size and she would be able to wear them for years to come, we should buy one of each color.

Well, not exactly all of them, but we did get two including a red, and a blue. Yael did wear them, at least once or twice a year on a cold winter day or for a costume party and occasionally to school. But for the most part, for years the "bargain boots" remained in mint condition in their original boxes in the closet.

Every year at the end of the winter, when the shoes and sweaters were packed away to make room for the summer sandals and shorts, they would be put away for the next year. Yael eventually married and moved out of the house, yet those boots remained in their original boxes in the closet in her room at the family home.

Years later, when she was almost thirty years old and we were making a major international move to Boston and downsizing, we all felt that it was time to part with the red and blue suede boots and to pass them on to someone who would enjoy wearing them. For some reason, all those years, even when Yael no longer wore the boots, it was difficult for me to part with them. Somehow, each winter when the boots were unpacked, they brought back memories of that wonderful year of her coming of age and of that schlopping trip that we shared together.

Savta Evelyn, age 82, in the 2000s

Sheryl: Savta Evelyn, as she is known to her grandchildren and great-grandchildren, had been in the late stages of Parkinson's disease for several years and had recently moved to a long-term chronic-care facility to be near us in Boston. Although she was mostly in a wheelchair, she was still able to walk with a walker and the help of a personal assistant.

The doctor recommended that we purchase a brand of shoes that would be more suitable for her condition at this stage of her life. A vendor who sells a specialty line of shoes with thick soles for an easier grip on the floor came to the nursing home with several models of these orthopedic shoes. Mom tried on a few pair of shoes and was not happy with any of them. She said, "They don't feel good and are not comfortable on my feet." The shoe salesman, perhaps the same Al Bundy that tried to sell shoes to Yael, tried to convince us that Mom would just have to wear them for a few days until she "broke them in" and then said, "They look nice and they will be fine." I felt such a sense of *déjà vu*: first my daughter and now my Mom being bossed around by a shoe salesman who thought he knew better than they did how their feet felt.

Mom was very persistent that they were not comfortable and that she did not want to purchase them. A few days later, we went to a shoe store that carried a different brand and Mom found a pair she liked. Although Mom emphatically said, "They look like old ladies shoes, but they are comfortable," she was willing to accept the fact that they would be a safer shoe when she was walking.

For years the roles have switched, as it often does with elderly parents, so that I have had to take on almost all the responsibilities. Mom needs 24/7 full-time personal care that includes bathing, dressing, and eating, and has not been able to take care of her finances for many years. She can no longer make many of her own decisions. However, when it comes to clothes and shoes, she is as alert as ever and knows exactly what feels right and is still able to tell us what she wants. My mom always had beautiful clothes, and as her personal schlopper, it is important to me that she continues to dress in a style that makes her look beautiful. The aids and nurses love dressing her and make sure that she is always color coordinated. She is known in the nursing home as the best dresser, and she still takes pride in how she looks.

Sheryl's Granddaughter, age 2, in the 2010s

Sheryl: Yael had just taken her four-year-old son to see the *Jungle Book* Broadway show. I knew that since my granddaughter and I would be together, I needed to divert her attention so that she would not see that her mommy and brother were going out without her. I asked if she wanted to go to Marshalls, and she got so excited that she got dressed and ready to go in no time. At about seven in the evening, just as the crowds formed around Fenway Park, the two of us started our trek to our favorite neighborhood store.

To say the least, it wasn't easy to push and maneuver her stroller through the crowds of people who gathered outside Fenway Park for Game Six of the American League Championship (which we won, and we then went on to win the 2013 World Series as well; what a year!).

We finally got to Marshalls and my granddaughter was so excited as I wheeled her into the store because she knew that the shoes were on the first floor. As soon as we got to the shoe racks, she wanted to come out of the stroller so that she could walk and personally look at the shoes. The actual shoes are on a top shelf for an adult to see, whereas the boxes are stacked below and within arm's reach of a child. She started to walk down the aisle and began to choose shoes by recognizing the pictures on the boxes, such as Dora, Hello Kitty, and some pink flowers.

She wanted the Dora shoes, and although they were light-up shoes that she would have loved, they looked a little too clunky and heavy for her dainty feet, so I tried to move her attention elsewhere. She tried on a few other shoes and said her emphatic "no" to each one until she saw the pink Hello Kitty tennis shoes. She put them on and was the perfect lady in pink, her favorite color, from head to toe, from shoes to pants to shirts. She refused to take the shoes off and continued wearing them as we schlopped for dresses and toys in the store.

When we got to the checkout counter I had to pick her up so that the cashier could scan the shoes, still on her feet. As soon as we left the store and started walking home, she said, "I want to go home to show Mommy and Daddy and my brother my new pink shoes and new purple princess dress."

The next day, we all gathered in the living room. She got all dressed up to give everyone her little fashion show. We needed to wait patiently until she chose her outfit, which included her new dress and, as usual, differently colored socks. While walking around and showing off her new outfit and shoes, she was the happiest kid on the block.

Sheryl's Grandson, age 4.5, in the 2010s

Sheryl: My grandson also has flat feet, and his parents decided to take him to a podiatrist to check out his condition. The doctor recommended that he wear inserts in his shoes even though his arches will always remain flat. Asaf had inserts as well when he was a child and hated them, but unlike me he did not try to ruin them, explaining, "I saw how long it took to prepare them." Back then, they molded a cast on his foot and prepared a plaster-of-Paris, clunky insert. While my grandson sat on a bed, the doctor took his shoe, measured his foot, molded the insert, and put the inserts back in his shoes. Once he put on his shoes he started running from side to side to see if they were comfortable and had a huge smile on his face.

The next step was to buy new shoes. They went to the New Balance store in Boston, and my grandson started to look at all the shoes on the shelves. He saw a pair of shoes that he liked, but they could not find his size, and so they continued on their journey while my grandson pointed to other shoes, saying, "I want this one, and this one, and this one," and Asaf showed him every shoe he pointed to. When a salesperson approached to see if he could help, all Asaf thought of was this chapter of this book, a draft of which he had read. He thought to himself, "Only my son knows what he wants and what feels right," and so he respectfully declined the salesperson's help.

They lucked out, and finally found the correct size in the style of the first shoe my grandson liked and he tried them on. Once my grandson put the shoes on, he started running from side to side to see if they were comfortable. Then he looked in the mirror and said, "They're cool! I want these." Then he said, "I don't want them. I want to try on these shoes," and pointed to a different pair. Asaf immediately gave him the second pair of shoes. After trying them on and running from side to side, he said, "No I don't want these! I want the first pair." He put the first pair back on and looked in the mirror and said, "This is what I want; I want to go home and show them to Mommy and Savta Sheryl."

When he came home, he immediately put the shoes on, did his little fashion show, and started running with a huge smile on his face. Asked whether he liked the inserts and new shoes, he said, "I love them. They're comfortable." Asaf noted that his schlopping trip for shoes with his son was successful due to listening to him, giving him his time and space, and trusting his judgment. What more can you ask from a father?

Schlopping Tips

- Listen to your kids and the elderly and trust that they know what they like and what is comfortable for them.
- Even if a person has difficulty communicating verbally, they can still tell you what they want: just look at their eyes.
- Allow everyone young and old, even a small child, the chance to choose and express themselves. Don't decide for them.
- You can never be in someone else's shoes. So if they say the shoe fits, let them wear it.

11. New Life, New Traditions

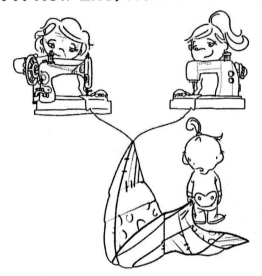

"Now we can go schlopping."

WHEN TWO LIVES INTERTWINE into one experience, a balance of benefits needs to take place. Whether you include the whole family in the experience or exclude everybody, the end result will be beneficial to all involved if the decision is made with compassion and love.

As a child, you start out with your immediate family, your parents and siblings, and several extended families, including maternal and paternal grandparents, aunts, uncles, cousins, and so on. Their traditions are your traditions that you may or may not pass on.

When you get married or have children, your immediate family expands and your responsibilities as well as privileges change. You go from being dictated the rules to dictating the rules and have the ability to create first and new traditions within your family. The million-dollar question is: When do you combine both your past and present immediate families and when do you include only your new immediate family in a family tradition? It is the balance between our own feelings and wishes and others' feelings and wishes that determine the answer.

Sheryl: From the time I was a young child, I imagined getting married in my mother's wedding dress in a garden wedding in the same way she did. My parents were married on Mother's Day in 1947, in a backyard garden wedding at her childhood home in Columbus, Texas. The ceremony took place under a *chuppah*, the wedding canopy, which my grandfather had decorated with flowers from his garden. The wedding dress was custom designed for Mom, and several years later her younger sister Maxine started a tradition by wearing the same dress as she walked down the aisle in the same garden. As a child, I always saw the wedding photos hanging on the wall at my grandparents' home and heard the stories about the magical weddings and dreamed of carrying on that same tradition. I just needed to find a husband, and from the day I met Sam, who was my friend's roommate at Tel Aviv University, I knew he was the one.

Growing up, I had seen the wedding dress only in pictures because it was stored in a closed box, labeled Wedding Dress, on the top shelf of the closet in my mother's childhood room and we were forbidden to open it up or even move the box. Gommie always told us, "We will take The Dress out ONLY when someone gets married." I finally saw it for the first time one month before my wedding. Unfortunately, it was not preserved well and the ivory white had turned slightly yellow and there were several stains that had never been removed. Perhaps if we had opened it years prior, even to take a slight peek, we might have been able to clean and preserve it properly.

Mom and I have very different body shapes, so I assumed that I would either alter the dress to fit or use the material to make another dress. Although the dress had faded and was too large in the bust and too long for my short torso, the only alteration I made was to shorten the front hem, as not to trip in the grass. Wearing my mother's wedding dress, in the original style, was more important than having a perfect fit. We had a lovely garden wedding in the backyard of Sam's aunt's home in Rehovot, Israel, surrounded by fragrant orange trees and catered by family and friends.

I told Yael stories about the family weddings and every few years, unlike Gommie, took the wedding dress out of the round white suitcase stored up in my closet and encouraged Yael to try it on. I loved watching her grow into it. I always told her, "You look beautiful in the dress, and I hope you will want to wear it for your wedding and carry on the family tradition." When it came time to plan her wedding, she made it clear that she did not want to wear The Dress, but instead wanted to buy her own, because, she said, "The Dress is old, yellow, stinky, and stained."

Before we went wedding-dress schlopping, Yael spent hours looking through bridal magazines and found a dress she loved from a specific bridal boutique, which was our first stop. As soon as we got to the shop, she requested the dress and went to try it on. As she stepped out of the dressing room, all I could say was, "Wow! You look radiant and beautiful." As I stood there watching my one and only daughter, in her chosen wedding dress, looking at herself in the mirror, all I could think of was, here is my baby, the daughter I nursed and nourished, and she is leaving our home to begin a new life with her love. Tears of joy and sadness swelled in my eyes.

Obviously, us being us, a decision could not be made without going to all the bridal shops and trying on dozens of other dresses. That day, we schlopped from store to store for more than seven hours, only to return to the first boutique, try on the first dress one more time, and reconfirm the "wow factor." Whether Yael finally chose the first dress due to the wow factor resulting from it being the first wedding dress she tried on, or whether she had already made her decision while going through the bridal magazines, or whether it truly was the perfect dress, it absolutely was beautiful and unique.

When we went wedding dress schlopping, I felt a bittersweet sensation. On the one hand, it was exciting to see my daughter trying on wedding dresses. But on the other hand, I knew that this schlopping trip meant she would not wear The Dress and would not continue a family tradition that I had so yearned for her to fulfill. Although I was sad she decided not to wear The Dress, I was thrilled that she had found her own perfect dress for her perfect day and that she had shared the schlopping trip with me.

A week before her wedding, Yael came to me and asked to wear the white and silver shawl that Gommie had hand-crocheted years before. It would be the "something old" and it would keep her warm at the after-party. I emphatically said, "No, I don't want it to get ruined." Yael was both hurt and insulted and asked, "What use is it if it just sits in the closet? Why are you keeping family things if we can't use them? Don't you want me to wear something special from the family on my wedding day? It's as if the family things are just for you and not for us." Later, Yael came to me and asked, "What if I wanted to wear your wedding dress? Would I be denied because you would be afraid that I would ruin it?" I replied, "That's something different. I have a great idea: Instead of wearing the shawl, why don't you change into my wedding dress for your after-party?" I just wanted to try to convince her one more time to wear The Dress. Yael asked, "So it's ok for me to maybe ruin the wedding dress but not the shawl?" I replied, "Well, it's already been worn several times, and it has stains on it, whereas the shawl is in perfect condition, handmade by Gommie, and I don't want it to get ruined." Yael replied, "You know what? Just forget it. I don't want to wear it. I'll find something else." After a few tense days, I finally realized how ridiculous it was to deny Yael the only family item she wanted to wear on her wedding day. When I approached her and gave her the shawl, I said only, "Please take care of it so nothing happens." Thinking back on this incident, I now realize how selfish I was, perhaps acting just like Gommie. It was as if the preservation of the garment, in the closet, was more important than passing a family item to the next generation.

Yael: After my baby girl was born, as I prepared for her naming ceremony, I read about a Jewish-Turkish tradition in which the mother sews a veil for her daughter and both mother and daughter stand under the veil throughout the ceremony until the name of the baby is finally revealed to the community. After the name is announced, the mother takes off the veil and saves it for her daughter for her wedding day.

The sewing of the veil felt right for me, and for this to be the first creation I ever made with my hands for my daughter. Although I did not hope or expect my daughter to wear the veil on her wedding day as the tradition entails, I did want to create something special from me to her to celebrate her life that I also hoped would become an important piece of family memorabilia. However, I had an internal conflict: I wanted to do it by myself, yet felt, rightly or wrongly, that my mom would want to take part in the making of the veil.

The conflict involved not only my mom's wishes and feelings versus my own, but also my thoughts about what my daughter might want. Would it be more special if the veil was only from her mom or from both her mom and her grandmother? How would I make the best decision? I knew there was no right answer and that no matter what I did, somebody might get hurt. If I did not include my mom, she would be hurt. But if I did not do it by myself, I would not wholly experience the joy and feeling of fulfillment resulting from making the veil and knowing that I had created something with my own two hands for my daughter.

I thought about what my mom would do and understood that she had seldom needed to battle with these types of dilemmas. She had left her parents when she was eighteen years old and had never lived near them again until her mother was elderly and moved closer to us so we could care for her. I thought that if she were me, she would have done it herself and would be talking about the item she made for years to come, as she did with all the outfits she sewed for her, my doll, and me when I was young.

Once I settled on the veil, we needed to shop for material. It was four days before the event, and my mom, my baby girl in a sling, and I went to buy materials. There was no discussion at this time about who would do what, and our first mission was just to find the fabric and the satin ribbon. The tradition is to use embroidered silk, and we thought we could find it in a local bridal shop. On the way, we stopped by the local Ben Franklin Store to stock up on sewing supplies; we bought a narrow white satin ribbon for the trim. We then went to the bridal shop, but they did not have embroidered silk, so we continued on our journey. We then crossed the street and went to a tailor, who recommended going to a fabric store in a nearby town. Whenever I pass that intersection, I have a smile on my face and think of that special schlopping day. We then drove to the fabric store but could not find embroidered silk. As we went through the stacks of fabrics and found an organza, white, see-through material with delicate pink flowers that reminded both of us of my wedding dress, we both knew it would be perfect for the occasion. As always, of course, we debated between two satin trimmings—a narrow pink or a wide white—for about two hours and eventually got the latter to add to the ribbon we had already purchased so that we could have three choices when we got home.

After we bought these fabrics, my mom came home with us. There was little time to finish this creation. I took all the fabrics out of the bags and spread them on the table. My mom started looking at everything, feeling the fabrics between her fingers, and, as usual, examining the quality and sharing with me what would need to be done.

It was at that moment that I made my final decision. I quickly weighed all the factors again from both sides. Three factors tipped the scale: first, the veil is traditionally sewn by the mother alone; second, my mom would have made it herself and not shared the experience with anyone, due either to circumstances or by choice; and third, every time I thought of doing it with her I felt sad and discouraged. This wasn't because I didn't like doing things with her. It was just because I wanted to give my daughter something special from me, her mother, as my mom had done for me so many times throughout my life.

I decided to be gutsy and told Mom I wanted to make the veil myself by explaining that I wanted to follow the tradition. I did not want to hurt my mom, although I know I did. But, acting like the great mom she is, she just smiled at me and said, "That's great. I didn't expect to be a part of creating the veil." We both knew that that was not true.

She gave me some pointers on how to embroider on lace, first printing the letters and tracing them with a pencil, and then suggested I should take it to a seamstress to get the lace and veil sewn together. She said, "If I had a sewing machine, I would do it myself. But unfortunately I don't have one now in our tiny apartment in Boston." It is her dream to have a sewing room again, and I hope she gets one soon.

I decided to hand-embroider my daughter's name, date of birth, and a special message from me in both English and Hebrew. The message was "May your life be filled with health, happiness, and love." It came out beautiful. I was actually surprised by how pretty it looked and so was my mom.

I was proud of the creation and was happy that I had the guts to do what I thought best. Although most feelings associated with the veil are positive, I still worry a little that I hurt my mom by creating this by myself, without her.

A few weeks after the ceremony, we discussed this issue and the following was her response:

Sheryl: Knowing the type of person I am—obsessive, a control freak, and a perfectionist—I knew that in order for you to be able to create the piece you wanted, I needed to step back. The only role I wanted to take in this process was to give you suggestions and show you sewing techniques. I knew also that this was a time for me to let go, because I will not be there always to help you make things for the kids. There are many things you teach your children as they are growing up; as a parent, I always wanted you to take things I taught you and incorporate them into your own tradition. Watching you holding on to your daughter under the veil was touching and unique and reminded me of the *chuppah* you stood under on your wedding day, which you had so beautifully designed. As with the veil, we both went schlopping for the fabrics, but you included others when making the *chuppah*. You gave your family and friends squares of purple and white satin, so that each could create a special message to you for your wedding day. Yotam and I took all of the squares and sewed them together in a quilt-like pattern around a purple velvet square that included the *Magen David*, the Star of David, the date of the wedding, your names in Hebrew and in English, and the biblical saying *Kol sason ve-kol simcha, Kol chatan ve-kol kalah* ("The sound of happiness and the sound of rejoicing, the voice of the bridegroom and the voice of the bride"). With the wedding *chuppah*, you wanted to include everybody, but with the veil, you wanted to do it all by yourself.

Things made with my hands were special things I could give to you, and it gave me absolute joy that you wanted to continue a tradition of making something with your hands to pass along to your daughter. You knew what you wanted, and I knew it was something you wanted to do by yourself. We shared it together through schlopping.

Yael: I guess the tradition of the veil was not only a new tradition that was started by me, but also an old tradition in disguise that was passed to me by my mom. She always used to sew for me and give me special things she created with her hands, and now I had done the same for my daughter.

At the time of making my decision about the veil, I also told myself that it was ok for me not to include my mom and to do it myself as I had already given her a great gift three weeks prior. Not only had I given her her first granddaughter, but also she had been present at the delivery of my new-born child.

Again, the decision-making process concerning whether Mom would join Asaf and me for the birth was made while weighing up all the people involved and the circumstances. As opposed to the veil, where I had several days to contemplate, this decision was made in a split second, while I was ten cen-timeters dilated, and within nine minutes of my baby's birth.

Without realizing it, I had given a present to my daughter as well as to my mom; she has another person with whom to share her coming-to-life experience. For a bed-time story, I often tell both my kids the story of "The Day You Were Born." It is one of their favorite stories and they can listen to it over and over again whether it is told by Asaf, me, or my mom. Since I was a child, my Mom always tells us the story of our births on our birthdays. Yotam and I used to laugh at her and say, "You told us the story already! Stop repeating it," although deep down we loved hearing it and hoped it would be told every year. As a child, I thought that birthdays were only about the person who had been born. Now, as a mother, I realize that it is also about the people who gave life to the person who was born.

My first birth was a magnificent emergency C-section that resulted in the most beautiful and healthy baby boy joining our breathing world. Holding him for the first time, looking into his eyes, smelling his body, and feeling him on my chest was happiness and life. It was funny to feel his elbows, knees, ankles, head, and buttocks and finally understanding which body parts I had felt when he was pushing in my uterus.

At week twenty-six of my pregnancy, my mucus plug came out, my cervix had shortened, and I started to experience con-tractions. I went to the hospital after I noticed bleeding, and they admitted me immediately. They said I needed to go on bed rest, and I took it very seriously. One of the best tips a nurse gave me was, "Now you stop being a pregnant woman and start being a parent. It is only your baby's interest that matters and nothing else."

I did not move for more than ten weeks, except for going to the bathroom, getting up to eat, and showering. My mother-in-law, Pnina, came from Israel to help out and was with us for more than eight weeks. I was practicing hypnobirthing, and instead of envisioning my uterus opening and relaxing, I envisioned it closing and uplifting. I was so afraid the baby would come out early that I was petrified to push when I pooped, and thus just let go and breathed it out without physically pushing it out. I was able to lengthen my cervix and keep my baby in for an additional ten weeks.

I did not want to purchase anything prior to the birth, nor did I want to window shop or shop online for the baby. All I concentrated on was making sure the baby stayed inside as long as possible. My way of coping with this worrying situation was not to prepare anything in advance and to linger on in the state of pregnancy as long as I could. The Jewish religion is very superstitious, and some parents do not purchase baby items or have baby showers prior to the birth. When a woman is pregnant in Israel, she can go to a baby store, choose the items she wants, put them on a list, but only pay for them and receive delivery once the baby is born.

After ten weeks, on a Friday, my doctor told me that I was fine and I could come out of bed rest. The first thing I wanted to do after leaving the doctor's office was to go schlopping for a stroller. We went to a store but stayed only a short while so I wouldn't exhaust myself. Being me, I of course did not purchase anything. Little did I know my baby would be born within sixteen hours and that that would be the last chance for me to shop and get ready before his birth.

On an amazing Saturday early morning in July 2009, I woke up to a wet bed, thinking my water had broken only to see I was in a puddle of blood. It was terrifying. We quickly drove to the hospital, and on the way Asaf said, "You know what day it is today? It's your son's birthday." I was excited and afraid for both his life and mine and told my husband, "It's not fair this is happening to us." He immediately replied, "It's not only your story. It is your son's story as well." After thinking of it like that, I understood that seeing that day as anything less than perfect would be shameful. And so I smiled and our beautiful journey continued.

We got to the hospital and I was attached to monitors immediately. I lost almost a pint of blood but was doing ok. Asaf and I agreed with the doctors that unless the labor process progressed and, as soon as there was the slightest sign of distress in the baby, a C-section must take place. After two hours, the distress signal came on the monitor, and I was taken to the operating room, received a back epidural, and was awake and alert for the birth of my son. He came out with the most beautiful dark blue eyes and red lips. After he was on me for a few minutes, they took him to be weighed and cleaned. Asaf looked at me with a question in his eyes: "What do I do, do I stay with you or go with him?" For the first time in my life I told him to leave me to go be with our baby. That was the second time I was a true parent.

And so, I was a first-time mom in the hospital after a C-section and had nothing for a newborn in my house. I needed to rely on Asaf, my mom, Yotam, and Pnina to purchase all the items before the baby and I arrived home. They went and bought clothes, blankets, a car seat, a stroller, diapers, toys, baby shampoo, baby lotion, and any other imaginable baby item. I wasn't even a part of the first schlopping trip for my son.

He needed to stay in the neonatal intensive care unit for a few weeks, and I had the "luxury" of going schlopping and choosing his coming-home outfit. I chose an orange-and-white-striped onesie with a little robot on it, which started another tradition in our family: it was the outfit both kids wore when they came home from the hospital.

Four weeks later, after he finally came home, we were able to have his *Bris*, circumcision ceremony. Asaf and I created a special ceremony that involved all the grandparents saying a special prayer. My mom crocheted a special blue and white *yarmulke* for my son, which she extends as he grows, and all the men wore the *yarmulkes* that my mom had crocheted for them for our wedding eight years before. Asaf and I needed to go schlopping for clothes for the *Bris* since nothing in my closet fit. I bought a beautiful white and black dress with a wide black belt at the waist and buttons on top, so that I could easily open my dress, without taking it off, to breastfeed my newborn.

The dress fit snuggly on my postpartum, womanly body, and I wore it again three years later for my law school graduation.

With my daughter, I had a different experience. Many doctors did not want me to attempt a VBAC, vaginal birth after caesarean. But my OB/GYN trusted my feeling about my condition and encouraged me to try. This time, Asaf and I opted for a doula, a birthing coach, to help with the decision making if needed, which, in retrospect, may have been a factor in my invitation to my mom to be part of the birth.

One day in August 2011, at 7:30 a.m., I woke up to a very intense contraction at the same time a 6.0-magnitude earthquake shook the local area. My doula as well as my doctor told me that this delivery would probably be slow and long as it would be my first "natural" one, so I labored mostly at home. I called Asaf at 12:15 p.m., after the contractions had become more frequent and intense. He asked if he needed to come home from the office or could wait until Yotam, also his business partner, came back from a meeting. I, being the no-worry gal, said, "Sure, it can wait. I'll call you if I need you." I then called my doula, who was in Boston visiting clients, and she said she would swing by around 2:00 p.m. to see how I looked.

I then got on my birthing ball and was swaying from side to side thinking about what I would eat before going to the hospital. At 1:15 p.m., after a deeper contraction and more intense pain in my buttocks, I called Asaf and said, "Come home *now*." When he arrived, he massaged my back and we talked about the restaurant we would go to before the hospital. When my doula finally walked in, at 2:15, she took one look at me and said, "You're fine. You look too comfortable: you still have many more hours, so take a walk and go eat. I'll go home, make dinner for my guests, and come back during the night or tomorrow when needed." I told her that my tolerance for pain is extremely high and that just because I looked comfortable did not mean that I was not progressing. I said, "If you leave now, you will probably miss it." So she stayed on a while longer. Little did we all know that the baby would arrive within two hours.

An hour later, I felt liquid coming out of my underwear and went to the bathroom to see what it was. It was blood. The doula looked at it and said, "It looks good and natural; your uterus is probably expanding and shifting. You're actually progressing very fast, so you better call your doctor." Although I was reassured that the blood was nothing to worry about, the experience I had had with my son was still with me, and I feared every contraction and bleeding.

After I called the doctor, who said I should go either to the office or the hospital to be checked, I decided that I needed a shower before I left the house and ordered Asaf to come into the bathroom with me. I washed my hair and brushed my teeth. Now I felt that the baby was coming. I took a twelve-minute shower and felt four contractions. My poor husband was screaming silently on the inside, "Are you mad? Get out of the shower and let's go to the hospital *now*," but out loud he said just, "We'll do whatever you want, baby." And so we gathered all our stuff and took the one thing we wanted, our video camera. On the way, I called my mom and told her,

"It's time; I'm going to the hospital. But I need a favor. Please go to Best Buy and buy a tripod because we want to video the birth of the baby."

We chose not to know the sex of the baby this time around, and on the drive to the hospital I turned to Asaf and said, "I think it's a girl." The reason was very superstitious and physical. I was nauseous with my second but not at all with my first; had a low belly with my second but high with my first, even though people on the street kept saying that a low belly is a boy and high belly is a girl. On the ride to the hospital, I just went into my body and felt that I had a daughter.

I arrived at the triage station in the hospital at what turned out to be just seventeen minutes before the birth and kept saying, "The baby is coming *now!*" My doctor said, "Babies don't come out that fast," but I was dilated ten centimeters when she checked me. She asked if I thought my water had broken. My instinct told me that it hadn't and she said I was right. She told me to go to the delivery room immediately and asked if I wanted a wheelchair. I said no as it was more painful to sit than to walk. But as soon as I started to walk down the hallway, my water broke. I said, "Oops! I think my water just broke; sorry for the mess." But I felt delighted to experience an aspect of delivery I had not experienced before. Everything was so fast that they did not even have time to put an IV needle in my arm as hospital procedure entails with a VBAC.

When I got to the delivery room and climbed onto the bed I got on all fours, like an animal, to alleviate the pain in my buttocks. I think due to my endometriosis, the pressure exerted by the baby's head was extremely painful. I asked for a mirror so I could watch the birth of my baby and see our bodies change from one to two. As they rolled the mirror into the room, my doula entered. Then a security guard told me, "Your mother is waiting outside." I knew she was there because she was waiting to give me the tripod. I looked at my doula in the room, and thinking of my mom outside, I said to myself, "How can I deny her this experience?" I asked Asaf if it was ok for my Mom to enter, and, loving husband that he is, he said, "Whatever you want, baby."

My mom came upstairs thinking she would give the tripod to the doula and leave and was astounded when they told her to walk into the room. She looked at me in confusion, and I said, "It's ok, Mom, you can stay. Just start filming." My mom did not expect to be part of the labor because I am a very private person. We also often spoke of whether a mother should be part of her daughter's labor experience and both agreed in the past that the birth of a child is one that only the parents should enjoy. We were wrong.

After a minute and in between two contractions, I asked my mom, "How did you shop so fast?" She replied, "I'm an experienced shopper. I know what I want and where to find it. When I need to, I can shop very fast and be in and out in a matter of minutes." I chuckled at the thought of my mom shopping so fast and envisioned her as a cartoon character running around in fast motion.

I used all my power, control, and muscles to focus on the baby and myself, and I used my voice to enhance my energy as is practiced in sports and martial arts. Asaf said I looked and sounded like the most powerful warrior he has ever seen.

Within nine minutes, I breathed my beautiful healthy baby out and saw that she was a girl, even before Asaf announced it. After smiling at Asaf with love and putting my newborn on my breast to feed, I looked at my mom with joyful tears running down my cheeks, and said, "Now we can go schlopping."

Schlopping Tips

- It is ok to do things on your own.
- A new tradition is often actually an old tradition in disguise.
- Letting go is as important as helping.
- Don't be afraid to try new things, because they will often enrich you and your loved ones.
- Schlopping is not only about what you buy but also about the people you do it with; it is about the relationships, self-image, and memories that are developed while shopping with a person you love.

12. The Hidden Secrets of

Schlopping™

"The next time you go out shopping, take a loved one and make that moment special."

THE SACRED RITUAL OF SCHLEPPING with someone you love while shopping should be cherished and nourished. Schlopping is a tool that can help us deal with life. It opens the channels of communication, allows loved ones to spend time together, and shapes our view of the world and ourselves. It helps us deal with tensions or disagreements, reveals our secrets or fears, and provides us the opportunity to gaze at ourselves and others in the mirror. It enables us to enter a different world and, for a moment, to escape our reality, reinvent our story, and re-energize ourselves. It also gives us the option to purchase an item and bring back a piece of memorabilia from the schlopping expedition.

Whether we love to shop or cringe at the idea of a mall, schlopping is a way to connect to our loved ones, ourselves, and our community. It is an activity that we do at almost every important milestone in life, as well as, on a daily basis, in a public, neutral place. Doing it with a loved one is what makes it unique, and the effect it has over the lifespan is what makes it important.

The next time you go out shopping, take a loved one and make that moment special. Whether you laugh, giggle, cry, fight, or resolve an issue, do it with compassion and love. Schlopping will strengthen your relationships, build your self-image, and create lifelong memories.

Glossary

Bar Mitzvah	ceremony for a Jewish boy when he takes on the responsibilities of an adult, age 13 (Hebrew)
Bat Mitzvah	ceremony for a Jewish girl when she takes on the responsibilities of an adult, at age 12 or 13 (Hebrew)
boob-self	accepting your breasts as they are
bris	Jewish covenant of male circumcision (Yiddish)

Chanukah	the Jewish festival of lights, also spelled Hanukkah
chevre kadisha	Jewish burial society (Hebrew)
chuppah	traditional marriage canopy (Hebrew)
chutzpah	audacity, nerve, gall (Yiddish)
dressing room talk	the conversations that take place in a dressing room
go-sais	the state of lingering between life and death (Hebrew)
Gommie	made-up family word for our grandmother
Kol sason ve-kol simcha, Kol chatan ve-kol kalah	the sound of happiness and the sound of rejoicing, the voice of the bridegroom and the voice of the bride (Hebrew)
latkes	potato pancakes; a traditional food for Chanukah (Yiddish)

Magen David	Star of David (Hebrew)
mazal tov	congratulations (Hebrew)
menorah	nine-branched candelabra used on Chanukah (Hebrew)
nosh	to eat or to munch on snacks (Yiddish)
Passover	holiday commemorating the Jewish people's exodus from Egypt
Passover Seder	the ceremonial Passover dinner during which the story of Exodus is told
Purim	holiday commemorating the salvation of the Jewish people in ancient Persia
Saba	grandfather (Hebrew)
Savta	grandmother (Hebrew)

schlep	to carry a heavy load and/or to go from place to place (Yiddish)
schlopping	the ritual of schlepping with someone you love while shopping
schlopping buddy	the person you take with you when you go schlopping
schlump	a sloppy person (Yiddish)
schvitz	to sweat (Yiddish)
self-mirror-monologue	the way you talk to yourself while you gaze in the mirror
Shabbat	Sabbath (Hebrew); celebrated from sundown on Friday until sunset on Saturday
shivah	the traditional seven-day mourning period; a mourner "sits shivah"
Shulchan Aruch	the code of Jewish law (Hebrew)

SSB	Shopaholic Symptoms and Behaviors
synagogue	Jewish house of worship
tallit	prayer shawl (Hebrew); tallis (Yiddish)
Thanksgivukkah	The name people gave the day in 2013 on which both Thanksgiving and Chanukah were celebrated
the American Terror Attack Walk	the walk that people do after a terror attack in America when all public transportation shuts down for hours
The Dress	the family wedding dress
The Fashion Show	the ritual of coming home after schlopping and trying on clothes
tshatshke	trinkets or knickknacks (Yiddish)

tumah	impure (Hebrew)
yarmulke	skullcap that Jewish men wear (Yiddish)
Yiddish	an Eastern European language based on German and Hebrew

.

About Us

Sheryl E. Mendlinger, Ph.D., is a daughter, wife, mother, and grandmother and has been part of a living four-generation lineage of women most of her life. She designed macramé jewelry and sold her creations in international art shows. She received her B.A. in English literature and linguistics and her M.A. and Ph.D. in education from Ben-Gurion University of the Negev, Beer Sheva Israel. Sheryl's academic expertise and publications are in understanding the inter-generational transmission of knowledge and health behaviors from mother to daughter in multicultural populations. She has worked for over thirty years in various universities as a program director and teaching professor in women's health, including in an educational program for undergraduate studies for men and women prisoners in Massachusetts. She currently works at The Institute on Urban Health Research and Practice at Northeastern University in Boston, MA. As a two-time breast cancer survivor, she became a promotional speaker and advocate for wellness through dragon boating and rowing. Sheryl loves to schlop, cook, knit, sew, swim, spend time with her family, and laugh.

Yael Magen, Esq., is a daughter, granddaughter, wife, and the mother of two young children. She is a graduate of Northeastern School of Law, Boston, MA and of Hebrew University, Jerusalem Israel in International Relations and Media and Communications. She has been a social organizer and a mayoral candidate and has worked in government and nonprofits that work to advance job creation and wealth generation. She ran for Mayor of Beer Sheva, Israel at the age of 26. Her legal practice in Boston, MA--Multigenerational Family Law and Taxes, LP--helps families that have physical, financial, and emotional responsibilities for two or more generations with finances and estate and other legal issues. Her hobbies include dancing classical ballet, writing songs, singing off key, spending time with her family, and schlopping.

Roxie Voorhees grew up in Coney Island, Brooklyn, and her small family can now boast five generations on the same block. She began her career with five years as a beach lifeguard. She holds a B.F.A. in Toy Design from the Fashion Institute of Technology and works in the toy industry. Roxie's interests include travel, snowboarding, wake boarding, surfing, bike riding, and architecture.